BEHAVIOUR TECHNOLOGY

In memory of
Titi
who introduced me to the study of psychology

Behaviour Technology

A new approach to managing people at work

Michael Wellin

Gower

Published by
Gower Publishing Company Limited
Aldershot, Hants, England

British Library Cataloguing in Publication Data
Wellin, Michael
    Behaviour technology.
    1. Personnel management
    I. Title
    658.3   HF5549

ISBN 0-566-02329-6

Contents

Preface

Business organisations in the 1980s face an unprecedented struggle for survival. Fiercer world-wide competition, scarce energy resources, recession and dramatic technological innovation all make the task of managing a business organisation increasingly demanding. Behaviour Technology is concerned with how managers can meet this challenge by making better use of the most critical (and increasingly the most expensive) resource available to them – people.

Many books have already been written on how to develop and utilise people in the pursuit of business objectives. Most of these have concentrated on the use of one particular technique or theory to solve personnel problems in organisations. In this book I do not present any magic formulas which will lead to the Nirvana of productivity, profitability and growth, as I don't believe there are any. Instead I have adopted an approach which has proved itself in many other fields. The approach is that of technology. In the place of pre-packaged solutions managers have available a vast data-base to assist them in solving their problems with people – data about how people behave at work. My aim in writing this book is to encourage managers to become more aware of the facts of behaviour, and thereby become more able to select and implement specific action plans which tackle the human resource problems they are facing.

Behaviour Technology has been written for the human resource specialist whether in personnel, training, or management/organisation development. Because of the concern with how human resources can contribute more to the success of the business I hope the book will also be of interest to the line manager.

Inspiration to write this book came to me during a break away from the industrial world, while trekking in the Himalayas. It occurred to me that remote mountain communities, like business organisations in the industrial world, are engaged in a struggle for survival. During the course of a few days my companion and I walked through a number of villages, some of which thrived, while others existed at subsistance level. As noticeable as the differences in wealth were the very real differences in behaviour of the villagers. Better off communities were characterised by behaviour which included markedly higher energy devoted to work and much greater collaboration than those villagers which were poorer. While it would be unrealistic to attribute wealth solely to work behaviour, the apparent connection between the two suggests more than a small degree of inter-dependence.

The contrast between more and less afluent Himalayan communities seemed to me to be analogous to that between more and less productive business organisations.

The most demanding task in writing this book has been to identify and use a suitable framework to categorise and describe the multitude of possible organisational behaviours. In particular I wanted a framework which does justice to the reality of our lives both as analytical problem solvers, and as feeling, sensing beings. Many established approaches to behaviour tend to concentrate on one of these to the exclusion of the other. To meet the need I integrated two established frameworks for describing and categorising behaviour — the Problem-Solving Dimensions for rational problem-solving, and Transactional Analysis for behaviour which expresses feelings.

After describing the principles of Behaviour Technology in the first two chapters, the remainder of the book concerns the application of these in a number of key human resource situations. Chapter 3 provides an overall analysis of a business meeting, with subsequent chapters addressing the problems of how to define job performance requirements, assessment interviewing, performance appraisal and improvement, working in groups, managing people, assessment centres, manpower development and conflict management. Each of these chapters reviews established thinking in these areas, and then looks at them from a Behaviour Technology perspective, often with specific behavioural examples which are analysed. The final two chapters are wider in scope, and address issues of when and how to implement Behaviour Technology.

A chapter relating Behaviour Technology to mainstream psychology was originally planned. Because of the book's emphasis on practical problem solving it was, however, decided to omit such a chapter, and instead concentrate on questions of application. The interested reader will in any case be able to make connections between BT and organisation psychology in the earlier parts of each chapter which deals with a specific application area.

I want to extend my thanks to the many people who have assisted and supported my efforts in putting this book together. First I want to thank Sue Selwyn, who encouraged me to bring back my Himalayan inspirations and translate them into reality over many weekends without a single complaint. Pam Pocock made an invaluable contribution in helping me get my initial ideas together on the format of the book, without which it would never have seen the light of day. Particular thanks also to Peter Hepple and Roger Pryor who reviewed my ideas on each chapter and added to them considerably. My thanks also to the many colleagues in BOC Engineering Division and ICL United Kingdom Division with whom I have worked, and who have contributed both directly and indirectly to my learning and development. Finally and by no means least my thanks to William Byham and the late Eric Berne for their frameworks for understanding behaviour.

M. W.

Introduction

Technology affects every part of our lives in industrial societies. While we may only consciously be aware of technology in the workplace, in the form of computers or unmanned manufacturing, it affects almost every-thing we do or experience. Electronic gadgetry in the home is now commonplace, whether it takes the form of the video recorder or the programmed washing machine. It equally affects outdoor leisure activities, even those which appear to be close to nature such as sailing or mountaineering. In both these sports technological breakthroughs in the development of new materials and fabrics have radically altered the nature of equipment and clothing.

THE CHARACTERISTICS OF TECHNOLOGY

Amidst our technological lives it is easy to lose sight of what technology really is. Irrespective of their field, all technologies share three funda-mental characteristics. The first is that they involve the application of a body of knowledge to solve problems. The second is that they take account of the facts surrounding a problem. The third is that they involve the development of specific solutions. A few examples of how these characteristics operate will indicate how important they are for our concept of technology.

One example which you may well have encountered is when a motor mechanic attempts to get a faulty car to start. Unless the mechanic is able to pinpoint the cause of the breakdown from talking to the owner, he (it might sometimes be a she though I haven't yet met one) will carry out a number of checks in an effort to identify why the car will not start. He may check whether there is sufficient fuel in the tank, and that it is being supplied to the engine. He may check whether the battery is operating normally, and whether a spark is being generated in the spark plugs. After a number of such tests the mechanic should be able to identify the nature of the fault. Through a sequence of checks and tests the mechanic will be fulfilling the first two characteristics of car repair technology — applying a body of knowledge to account for the facts of the problem. Once the mechanic has diagnosed the fault he will then proceed to repair it, and/or to replace components so that the car can function normally. The repair of the car will be tailored to the particular fault diagnosed, rather than entailing the replacement of all parts or systems. This will thus fulfil the third characteristic of technology — adopting specific solutions to solve particular problems.

If the mechanic were to replace the complete engine whenever your car broke down, the car would be unnecessarily expensive to run. You might even find the fault had not been rectified. If the reason the car failed to start was due to a fault in the fuel line from the petrol tank, no amount of replacement of engine components would cure the fault. An assumption we make about all repair mechanics is that they adopt the three characteristics of technology in their work; they have a knowledge of the equipment, they identify the precise facts of why the piece of equipment is faulty, and they undertake specific repairs or replacement of parts which rectify the fault. It is when we suspect that the car mechanic has not followed these three principles that we find ourselves in heated arguements with the garage manager.

The three principles of technology are well demonstrated in industrial organisations. When computerising an accounting procedure the systems analyst will first attempt to understand the nature of the system to be computerised, and only then specify hardware and software which will enable this to occur in a cost effective way for the business. Similarly the factory engineer will take account of the precise nature of manufacturing requirements when proposing the purchase of new automated machine tools.

Whichever branch of technology we are involved in, we find that problem-solving involves the use of a body of knowledge, identification of the facts of the problem, and then the development of tailor-made solutions.

ARE THE APPLIED BEHAVIOURAL SCIENCES TECHNOLOGY?

Human behaviour, including organisational behaviour has long been the subject of psychological investigation, and this has resulted in the creation of a body of knowledge. Much of this knowledge, however, has remained at an academic level, and resulted in little real problem-solving in industry.

To date most organisations have only derived marginal benefit from the applied behavioural sciences. During the 1960s and early 1970s many managers became aware of the concept of motivation, particularly through the work of Maslow[1] and Herzberg *et al.*[2]. Despite the large amount of discussion this generated, the number of organisations which were able to use these concepts to solve bottom-line business problems were few. The extent to which organisations were able to decrease labour turnover, increase productivity, reduce the number and intensity of industrial disputes, or improve selection effectiveness as a result of this new-found knowledge is marginal. While there are some fascinating case studies quoted in the literature, the number of organisations which have derived tangible returns from the use of motivation theories are few.

The subject of leadership received much attention during the late 1970s. Efforts to change the quality of leadership, such as those based on Blake's 9.9. style[3] or Likert's System 4[4], all achieved great prestige for a time, only to be ignored not very long afterwards.

The bombardment of instant packaged solutions to assist in increasing human resource effectiveness appeared to be constant. To the non-expert manager, who was charged with achieving results through his or her subordinates, the effect must have been more than a little confusing. If a squirt of motivation failed to solve a particular problem, with a subordinate he might try more Theory Y, and if this proved unsuccessful then attendance on a Gestalt personal goals workshop might be tried. If none of these magic solutions worked, the manager could always revert to the traditional formula and fire the subordinate.

If we stand back from the details of most applied psychological theories and frameworks we realise that their approach is non-technological. The nature of many of the models put forward involves predetermined solutions, and is therefore highly limited in approach. By focusing on motivation our attention is diverted from the full facts of employee behaviour. When we adopt a leadership perspective we are equally considering only one factor which determines industrial behaviour and performance.

The result of this narrow perspective is that we become constrained from viewing the totality of what people do, and what determines it. Only when we take account of all the facts of how people behave can we be in a position to change their performance and behaviour. By looking at issues of motivation our attention is directed towards things that go on inside people's heads and away from what is happening in specific situations. If we look at leadership our attention is usually drawn away from the behaviour of subordinates to the behaviour of only one person in the group, namely the leader. By attending to wider relationship issues between employees, we are in danger of forgetting about issues concerning the individual skills and abilities which employees apply in their work. A fundamental weakness of many of the approaches adopted for solving human problems in organisations is that they divert attention away from the total facts of individual behaviour, and concentrate rather on only one or two narrow aspects of it.

When it comes to the adoption of specific action steps to solve a problem we are also likely to find the various models and frameworks restricting. Many of these offer ideal solutions which cannot be applied to actual profit-directed organisations. The assumption made by enthusiasts of Maslow's framework is that we need to harness the motives at the top end of the hierarchy of needs. Enthusiasts of the Herzberg approach will emphasise the need to adopt 'motivator' type solutions in an attempt to improve output. How the practising manager adaps and uses these ideas to solve a specific problem is an altogether more difficult question. More often than not the manager has to solve this all-important question with little more than some generalised principles. Similar criticisms apply to issues of leadership, which is considered in detail in Chapter 8.

By restricting attention to a limited aspect of a human problem, often with little help on how to gather data on its precise nature, many applied behavioural science models make it impossible for the manager to adopt a truly technological approach. Instead of having a tool bag to diagnose the precise issues in the problem, and then select an action plan for tackling it, the manager finds himself ill-equipped and unaided. Actually, managers find that their personal experience and intuition provide a better guide to solving human problems than the various behavioural science models. The validity of this conclusion is well supported by the infrequent use made of the behavioural sciences by business organisations facing problems in the current recession.

THE OBJECTIVES OF BEHAVIOUR TECHNOLOGY

The emphasis of this book is on a technological approach to using human resources effectively for the creation of industrial wealth. It proposes a reorientation and adaptation of the body of knowledge of industrial and organisational psychology. In the place of mechanistic and impractical models and theories, Behaviour Technology postulates that the manager will become most effective in human problem-solving if he or she concentrates on the facts of employee behaviour, and tailors problem solutions to these.

Behaviour Technology shares the characteristics of other technology forms. The approach adopted by car repair technology or computer technology, of identifying the full facts of the problem before developing specific solutions, can be utilised as effectively by a manager tackling a human resource problem. Instead of looking to the in-vogue behavioural theory, the manager has the option of concentrating on the facts of the problem he is facing, and then formulating and implementing unique action steps which will lead to increased effectiveness.

The results of psychological research have provided many useful ideas and approaches to the way we think about people at work. It is proposed to use these insights in a way that enables managers to take charge over the specific problem situations they are faced with. The structure of the chapters in Part Two has been influenced by prevailing thinking and methods in organisational psychology. Rather than accept these results as they stand, however, each chapter will provide a reorientation of accepted thinking within a Behaviour Technology context. Behaviour Technology in common with other technologies holds that there are no standardised 'off the shelf' solutions to problems; I will emphasise the uniqueness of each situation and its implications for problem-solving.

The impact of a technological approach to human problem-solving could be equivalent to that of any other new form of technology. One example of how advanced technology can radically alter our approach to understanding and then solving problems is fish farming. If we want to catch a few fresh water trout a suitable rod, line and bait will be sufficient as long as we fish in a suitable location. If our need for trout increases we might be able to satisfy our requirements by using the same technology but simply using two or three rods simultaneously; perhaps inviting our friends to set up rods along the river bank to help us increase our catch. However, if other people were competing with our efforts to catch fish we might find the river banks lined with fishermen, all trying to catch the limited number of trout that were available. In such circumstances many fishermen would be disappointed, as the competition would result in too few trout to go round. Alternative strategies would therefore become necessary. One radical solution to the problem of increasing the supply of trout would be to set up a fish farm for breeding and catching trout. The traditional rod and line method of fishing would then become redundant for providing trout cost effectively, once the fish farm method was adopted.

The difference between rod fishing and fish farming extends beyond the mere scale of operations. Fishing with a rod and line relies on a simple one-off intervention with nature; knowing which time of year and which river is best for fishing, and then using the line and bait. In marked contrast to this approach, fish farming relies on a comprehensive understanding of the life cycles and habitat of the trout. It involves the creation of a special environment where fish can best breed and mature. Successful fish farming requires an active intervention with nature, based on detailed knowledge. In contrast the rod and line fisherman can remain largely ignorant about the growth and life cycles of the trout, so long as he knows how to use a rod and line.

The application of Behaviour Technology can create a radical change in the methods adopted by industry to solving human problems. Instead of relying on one-off mechanistic models about people (equivalent to the rod and line fisherman's knowledge about trout), Behaviour Technology encourages managers to view human problems in their widest and fullest sense. Industry to date has paid relatively little attention to the uniqueness of human resources in industry and commerce. Although many companies now have personnel departments and many managers and supervisors receive training in man management, organisations today are at the same stage of human management as the solo fisherman with his amateur rod and line.

THE CASE FOR BEHAVIOUR TECHNOLOGY

The introduction and application of any new form of technology has always needed justification. Experience of some advanced technologies suggests that their results may not be entirely beneficial to society. In the case of nuclear technology the benefits for society are more than open to question. The benefits derived to date from the peaceful application of nuclear technology are certainly not beyond question even from an economic point of view, as demonstrated by the continuing higher cost of producing electricity by nuclear methods compared to more conventionally fuelled power stations. In the United States and Europe the set-up costs of nuclear power plants are spiralling at a rate which makes the completion of many half-built power plants uneconomic, despite current price levels of oil and other fossil fuels. If we take account of the possibility of a world nuclear holocaust as a result of the development of the atomic bomb, the case for nuclear technology becomes still more debatable.

While the negative aspects of Behaviour Technology could in no way be compared to those of nuclear technology, the case for its wider introduction nevertheless needs to be made. The justification proposed here stems from the increasing difficulty business organisations face in attempting to survive in our economic and social environment.

Enterprises throughout the industrial world today face greater threats than ever before. The race to provide consumers with quality products at the right price is proving ever more difficult to businesses in Europe and America. Business organisations are being threatened not only by competitors on the other side of the world, but also by new product innovations, automated manufacturing methods, and resistance to change from within the enterprise itself.

One of the apparent characteristics of organisations that thrive and grow is their ability to harness and exploit advanced technology forms. The supremacy of American and British automobile makers earlier this century was to a large extent attributable to their application of flow line manufacturing methods. By standardising production and achieving greater division of labour, vehicle manufacturers were able to reduce costs significantly. The firms that thrived in the 1970s such as IBM, Hitachi, and VW all utilised the latest technology both in the products they manufactured and in the manufacturing methods themselves.

Recent moves towards the unmanned factory and automated office, made possible by the latest technological advances, promise quantum leaps in productivity. All the evidence suggests that those organisations which exploit these technologies will survive, while those that fail to do so will go to the wall.

A classic case in point is the British motor cycle industry. In the mid-1960s this industry had approximately 70 per cent of the world share of the motor cycle market; a decade later its share had been reduced to less than 10 per cent. On one level it is clear that British firms were too slow in updating their designs and too steeped in craft manufacturing technology. At another level of analysis, the failure of these firms can be attributed to the behaviour of their staff. What did the managers and employees of these firms fail to do which ultimately led to their bankruptcy? Part of their deficiency may have been a lack of understanding of world markets for their products, and of modern manufacturing methods. This may be due to a lack of initiative in looking outside the factory gates to see how the world was changing. Perhaps the style of management in these companies stifled creativity and innovation, and encouraged employees to do as they were told rather than to propose new and better ways of doing things. It may have been the value placed by management on conformity to established practices, instead of a willingness to do things differently or even to aim for different objectives, which led to these organisations being left behind in the industrial race.

After the event it is difficult to arrive at precise conclusions on why the behaviour of management and employees resulted in their firms being driven to the wall. The one fact that has been established with certainty is that whatever their behaviour, it was inappropriate to ensure their survival against overseas competition.

Inability to keep up with advanced technology does not just apply to old established organisations operating in traditional market places. The large mainframe computer companies are now experiencing increasing competition from small manufacturers of mini and micro computers which are able to offer cost effective solutions to industry. Within a few years the micro/mini computer market has grown from nothing to 30 per cent plus of the computer market, and will no doubt continue to grow during the 1980s. Unless the large mainframe manufacturers are able to offer equally cost effective products they may well find themselves increasingly under the same kind of threat as the British motor cycle industry; the threat from alternative suppliers who are able to offer a more compact, user friendly and cost effective solution, which is produced on the most up to date manufacturing technology.

Evidence suggests that one of the keys for unloocking the door to meeting customer needs innovatively is to take fuller account of the human factor. In a comparison between Japanese and British factories

Ronald Dore[5] found very striking differences in supervisory behaviour towards shop floor workers. The British factories studied by Dore had a very low rate of growth, even though management viewed their aim as profit maximisation. Supervision occurred through emphasis on subordinates fulfilling their job roles and responsibilities, largely on the basis of threats of sanctions for non-performance. Shop floor operatives in turn viewed management as exploitative, and resisted their authority where possible. In contrast Japanese firms in the same industry had very high growth rates and were doubling in size every three and a half years. Supervisory styles in these firms emphasised team work, with senior managers viewing their role as elders of a corporate community. Supervisors and managers concerned themselves with the well-being of individuals, and used exhortation as the prime method of exercising authority.

It would be inappropriate to attribute the growth rates of the Japanese firms solely to managerial and supervisory styles. Nevertheless the study lends weight to the notion that there may be some relationship between managerial and supervisory behaviour and organisation growth. The argument is reinforced by the apparent success of Japanese companies operating in parts of Britain where labour is notoriously difficult to manage and resistant to change. It might just be the case that by paying more attention to the uniqueness of the human factor, Japanese organisations are more able to innovate in terms of product design and manufacturing processes. For our purposes the important conclusion from Dore's work is that Japanese supervisory practices appear to take more account of the personal and emotional needs of employees, as well as their problem-solving and productive abilities.

Behaviour Technology, then, involves the utilisation of facts about how people behave for the solution of human resource problems. Instead of being concerned with ultimate truths about organisational behaviour, it concentrates on problem-solving. Behaviour Technology is a pragmatic approach to organisational behaviour which adopts a technological perspective. In the place of prescriptive models, which will inevitably become obsolete and outdated, Behaviour Technology encourages managers to become more aware of the facts of the human problems they are dealing with. Only when these are established to an adequate degree can the manager be in a position to improve effectiveness and performance. The technological approach is already well understood and applied in other functional areas, and with other resources in industry; it is however an approach which has rarely been applied to human resources.

REFERENCES

1) Maslow, A. H., *Motivation and Personality*, Harper and Row, 1954.

2) Herzberg, F., Mausner, B. and Synderman, B.B., *The Motivation to Work*, Wiley, 1959.

3) Blake, R.R. and Mouton, J.S., *The Managerial Grid*, Gulf, 1964.

4) Likert, R. *New Patterns of Mangement*, McGraw Hill, 1961.

5) Dore, R., *British Factory—Japanese Factory*, George Allen and Unwin, 1973.

PART ONE
PRINCIPLES OF BEHAVIOUR TECHNOLOGY

1   What is Behaviour Technology?

Behaviour Technology involves the collection and use of systematic behaviour data to tackle and solve human resource problems. The approach has potential value on a personal therapeutic level, and also in industry, which is the concern here.

Quantities of literature have been produced on the application of the behavioural sciences to problem-solving, but a review of this work is likely to lead to disappointment for the practitioner. Whether our prime concern is curing psychotics or maximising the effectiveness of a production department, the majority of the literature provides relatively little practical guidance on problem-solving. Often the main concern is the creation of schematic models and theories which explain why a person behaves in a particular way, but which prove of little value for gathering factual data to assist in changing that behaviour.

In contrast to the car mechanic discussed in the Introduction, many applied behavioural science solutions seem to pay relatively little attention to the real facts of what people do. Despite the fascinating theories of the unconscious developed by Freud[1], it was not so much these which helped to cure patients but rather Freud's open, non-threatening relationship with them which enabled them to become aware of their unproductive behaviours and feelings, and thereby make decisions to change. For practical purposes the theoretical framework of the Id, Ego, and Superego made only a marginal difference to the client (or, as Freudians refer to them, the patient). What did help clients was the opportunity to discuss their difficulties, without fear of criticism or censure. The support provided by Freud and his psychoanalytic followers by reflecting back to clients what they experienced and felt made possible the road to more adaptive behaviour patterns.

The questionable scientific validity of the psychoanalytic model has often been mentioned, but this is mainly of interest to academics. Despite the intense opposition of many 'behaviour therapists' to the psycho-analysts, it is curious how many of their case histories include reference to long and elaborate discussions with the patient, as well as to 'stimulus-response' based treatment. Perhaps many of the successes of both psycho-analysts and behaviour therapists have nothing to do with their theories, but rather are the result of the technology they use; providing people with an unrestrained non-critical supportive relationship with someone with whom they can explore their problems. While the field of clinical psychology is not our primary concern, the issue of technology as used by the therapist demonstrates well the concerns of Behaviour Technology.

In the field of industrial or occupational psychology vast numbers of theories and ideas have come and gone, rather like Paris fashions. For a short time they come into vogue, and then pass away into oblivion. However, when we ask how much these theories — for instance motivation theories — actually contributed to increasing business effectiveness, we are likely to become disillusioned. The reason for this is not that people do not have needs and desires which they seek to satisfy at work. On the contrary, we all have a vast array of needs which we carry with us wherever we are, including our workplace. The issue is rather that in the midst of the euphoria about new insights into motivation, few vehicles were provided for the practising manager which enabled him to harness simply and efficiently the motives of his subordinates towards the achievement of business goals. Given that most managers are unable to change radically the remuneration system of their organisations, the problem of harnessing people's motives to increase effectiveness is beset with problems. Reluctantly we have to conclude that the motivation theories, including the more recent ones which take account of expectations, failed to help managers examine the facts of employee behaviour, which are the only real data available for a manager to work with in solving human problems.

Similar experiences have occurred with regard to leadership. The early experts in this area preached participation in decision-making as the salvation for industrial problems. Exciting as this was to the liberal mind, it flowed against the whole idea of traditional authority in organisations. Even today the concept of the boss telling his subordinates what to do reigns supreme, and most of us will do as we are directed if after attempts at persuasion the order is merely repeated. The original participation approach to leadership became modified in the 1960s and 1970s. The theories took many forms, but essentially proposed that managers needed to take account of the task requirements as well as the human requirements at work. Perhaps the best publicised of these was the Managerial Grid of Blake, which encouraged effectiveness through the use of the 9.9. style (paying high attention to both people and task).[2]

These theories in turn were replaced by the contingency approach, initiated by Fiedler back in the 1960s,[3] and later developed by Reddin[4], which proposed that the optimum style depended on factors in the work environment which require a particular balance between concern for people and concern for task.

Intellectually these theories are highly appealing, and no doubt helped managers to develop greater sensitivity to the way they managed subordinates. Despite this mass of research (leading to tons of publications), the new theories had relatively little impact on industrial output. This is not to dismiss the instances where apparently worthwhile increases in output where achieved through developing and changing management styles, but rather to emphasise that these were the minority of cases. We have reluctantly to acknowledge that the practical result of most leadership training and development is marginal, despite the hopes of many of us, including myself, who were involved in it.

Other areas of applied behavioural science, including the total organisation development schools and individual interpersonal skill training, will not be evaluated in this chapter. Suffice it to say, however, that the practical impact of most of these has also been slight.

This conclusion raises the fundamental question of why so much well intentioned research and management effort resulted in marginal changes in performance. Many plausible reasons could be put forward. It might be argued that I am being unduly pessimistic and that many of these theories have made a larger and more enduring impact on industrial performance than I have suggested. The data on industrial disputes, resistance to technological innovation, poor decision-making, and alienation of large numbers of the working population suggest, however, that this is not the case. Your own evaluation of this question will be influenced by the extent to which behavioural science ideas, theories and techniques have contributed to the organisations in which you work. Even if your firm does use these, is the performance achieved significantly better than it would be if they were not used?

IMPRESSION FORMATION

When you last made a recruitment decision, what facts did you have available to indicate that the person you chose was the right man or woman for the job? To what extent did you know that they had the necessary technical skills to perform the job, or that their typical work behaviour would blend well with those of their colleagues, bosses, and subordinates? Even if they did convince you that they had been successful in their previous job, to what extent was this a valid predictor that they could effectively perform the job your organisation had to offer?

It is fashionable to joke about the use of stereotypes in assessing people, such as that glasses and a large forehead indicate intelligence, or that bright coloured ties and check suits indicate extroversion or an outgoing temperament. We may also believe that a firm handshake indicates a balanced and emotionally sound individual. There may even be some slight statistical correlation between these indicators, but, because of individual variation, to use them as methods of assessment will be highly misleading. Few managers need to be convinced of the very questionable validity of these popular sterotypes. Nevertheless reflection on the data used to make assessment decisions frequently suggests that it is of almost as flimsy a kind.

If you conclude that someone can work easily with people, how many pieces of information do you use to support this evaluation? Is it just that the person keeps telling you in the interview that they get on easily with everyone, or that they like their present boss? Or is it simply that you personally like them, and therefore assume that they would get on well with people? Perhaps you use non-work indicators, such as membership of a theatre group or local community group, as valid evidence. The objective information used to support decisions about an individual's ability to get on with people is often slight. And even if we have obtained a large number of examples which support the conclusion, we may be left asking whether getting on with people is really essential for effective job performance. Perhaps after all it is not so important, and what is required is that the individual can relate moderately well to achieve satisfactory job performance.

Communication experts suggest that more than 50 per cent of what is communicated between individuals occurs non-verbally,[5] in other words through body language, gesture, facial expressions, eye gaze, and posture. If this is accurate it raises the question of the extent to which we evaluate people, whether for appointment, promotion, merit award, disciplinary procedure, etc., because of non-verbal cues, rather than demonstrable results or verbal performance. This is a startling thought and may well challenge our belief in our own effectiveness as an assessor of people, based on hard data. Your reaction to this may well be sceptical — after all you have probably been trained at some stage in interviewing. Despite this, ask yourself how many pieces of objective information you had to support your evaluations of the last person you interviewed — is it on one dimension, on three or on ten dimensions? You may have even made your assessment before the candidate entered the room, based on the application form or personal recommendation, and merely used the interview to confirm your decision. Many interviewers, for example, ask about school examinations passed by a candidate, when this information is clearly written on the application form.

In contrast to the recruitment/appointment situation, consider the basis on which you decide whether someone you meet socially for the first time is the kind of person you would like to meet again. More than likely your decision will be based on how you felt about that person; that you felt good in their presence, that you got along, or that they were on the same wavelength as you. For many of us the decision to meet someone again will not be the subject of intense analysis. Rather we will arrive at a decision, often spontaneously, and initiate a further meeting.

We make many of our judgements and assessments of people on the basis of our own reactions and assumptions rather than tangible verifiable facts. If you were asked to list five features which characterise the behaviour of your husband, wife or one of your parents, you could no doubt do so readily. Could you then back up your assessment of these characteristics with examples of specific behaviours which support your assessment? Try this exercise before reading further. You may well find it more difficult than you imagine.

The exercise you have just tackled referred to someone you know very well, and have spent a lot of time with. How easily could you do the same for a colleague at work, or someone you only meet occasionally on a social basis? More than likely you would find it difficult to identify three tangible examples of that person's behaviour which demonstrate or support the five most important characteristics you attributed to them.

If you attempt the same exercise jointly with a work colleague on someone you both know quite well, you may find it interesting to compare the data you both produce to support the same alleged behaviour characteristics, e.g. sociability, initiative, emotional stability, planning ability, etc. Tackling this type of exercise with another person, even when you both clearly know and agree what you mean by these labels, can shed much light on the way we make judgements about others.

In many cases our assessments of others are influenced largely by our own experiences. Whether we assess people as intelligent or unintelligent often depends on how much weight we put on this attribute. Equally when we assess someone as friendly and warm, as opposed to cold and aloof, this is heavily influenced by our personal desire to be with people who show warmth.

Our psychological makeup will in part be influenced by the culture in which we live. A man who hugs every male whom he knows well and whom he hasn't seen for a few weeks would be considered eccentric by most British people, while in Egypt this behaviour would be considered completely normal; conversely a Japanese adult will greet his or her parents after a separation (even of months or years) by bowing to them, rather than hugging or kissing them. So the dimensions on which we evaluate others, as well as the data we may select to demonstrate their grading on these dimensions, is to a high degree influenced by our psychological makeup rather than by any external reality.

Most of the time the evaluations and assessments we make of others happen spontaneously and without too much conscious thought. Many of our assessments frequently take place without effort or even evaluation of data; we just arrive at a decision, apparently automatically. It is more rare for people carefully and painstakingly to take account of the objective information they have about someone before making an assessment. The exceptions are those whose work is concerned with making professional assessments, including personnel specialists, psychotherapists, and those in the caring professions.

Our assessments of others tend to be made in a hierarchy, ranging from automatic reactions to systematic data collection. At the one extreme we merely decide that we like someone and feel positive about them, or that we dislike them and feel hostile or bad about them. At the other extreme are those assessments made for professional purposes which attempt to ignore the 'feeling factor' and are (supposedly) based purely on objective information about behaviour or performance, e.g. ability to complete a specific task within a specified time. Most of our day to day evaluations of others tend to be based more on reactions than on objective information.

This may seem preposterous, and to suggest that you are not a rational person. Reflect, however, on one recent face to face conversation you had with another person which lasted for more than ten minutes. It could have been with a member of your family, a work associate, or a social acquaintance. Recall the outcome of your discussion and how you felt about that person after the conversation. Did you feel positive, happy, sad, confused or bored? Once you have got in touch with the dominant feeling, consider the context in which your communication took place. How did your non-verbal communication express how you both felt?

NON-VERBAL BEHAVIOUR

Non-verbal communication (NVC) occurs continuously, wherever we are, and whoever we are with, and the next few paragraphs summarise the main types. As you read through them attempt to relate these to your memory of and reflections on the ten-minute conversation you just recalled.

Spatial positioning sets the scene for non-verbal communication and refers to the proximity between people, territorial behaviour and movement within a physical setting. A discussion in an office with a desk sets certain constraints on where and how the occupants may sit, as do tables in a restaurant or furniture in our lounge. The physical environment nevertheless can be manipulated to suit the type of interaction we intend to have. Physical distance is a factor which, from the beginning of a meeting, indicates the tone it is likely to take. It has been suggested[6] that there are four distance zones used by North Americans: public, over twelve feet; social-consultative, nine to twelve feet for more impersonal relations; personal, eighteen inches to four feet for close relationships; and eighteen inches or less for intimate relationships. Even within the formal constraints of an office we choose the distance we wish to sit from another person by selection of which chair to sit in, or by moving the chairs to suit our convenience, or even by choosing to ignore the chairs and sitting on a table or standing up. With people with whom we have established relationships, some informal proximity rules or arrangements usually exist. Mostly we have an agreed position which we take at home in the lounge with our husbands/wives, or in the office with the boss. When a stranger comes into the lounge our seating positions will be different.

Our positional orientation towards others also indicates our feelings towards them. Side by side positions are regarded as co-operative, while directly facing positions can be either competitive or intimate.

Reflect for a moment on the ten-minute conversation you had, and consider the initial spacial positioning taken up by both of you, and whether this changed. Did you start off at a distance and get closer, or start close together and move apart? Were you predominantly facing one another or side by side?

Posture is another important method of non-verbal communication and reflects how we relate to others as well as our emotional state. Positive feelings are indicated by leaning forwards, and openness of arms and legs. Relaxed posture, i.e. sideways leaning, asymmetrically placed arm and leg positions, and muscle relaxedness are adopted towards those we like and also those of lower status. On the other hand a level head, arms by our side and feet on the ground suggest a logical and reasoned state. Slumped shoulders and head angled downwards usually denote passivity and helplessness, while folded arms and stiff bearing with head angled upwards tend to suggest control, critical opinions, and restriction.

Reflect briefly on the postures you and the other person held in that ten-minute conversation. Was the other person sitting with asymmetrical arm or leg positions, or were they tightly held to his or her body? Was his or her head angled up or down or was it level? These indications will tell you much about the state of the other persons during your conversation.

Facial expression and gaze provide other indicators of how we feel. Research by Osgood[6] suggests that at least seven clearly different emotions can be expressed and recognised from facial expression; happiness, surprise, fear, sadness, anger, disgust, contempt and interest. Field experiments (i.e. situations which closely resemble real life) suggest that the arousal of specific emotions in people gives rise to consistent facial patterns. Happiness is for example indicated by open lips with raised and retracted corners of the mouth, dilated nostrils, and depressed upper eyelid with wrinkled lower lid. Length of gaze and pupil size are also indicators of liking. We tend to look more often at people we like, and enlarge our pupils when looking at people or objects we are attracted towards. Dominance of one person over another is suggested by the lower status person gazing more at the high status dominator than the other way round. Avoidance of gaze frequently indicates negative emotions such as anxiety, shame, or embarrassment. When we are afraid we tend to freeze our eyes open, while in anger the eyes are narrowed.

Reflect on the facial expressions and gaze patterns you noticed during your ten-minute conversation. This may be more difficult than recalling the verbal behaviour you both exhibited, but you may be able to recall at least some of the facial expressions of the person you were with. Did they smile, laugh, look at you or away from you most of the time? Did you exchange many mutual gazes at one another's eyes? The facial expressions of the person certainly transmitted powerful signals to you about how they felt about your interaction.

As a result of considering the spatial setting, body movements and facial expressions during your ten-minute conversation you will have become much more aware of precisely what occurred during that transaction, and how you and the other person behaved. Could it be that the real meaning of that conversation was expressed predominantly by your non-verbal communication, and that the words merely added to the richness of what was expressed? You are unlikely to have been able to recall all the non-verbal communication that took place or all that exhibited by the other person. It is even more difficult for us to be aware of our own non-verbal communication, but whatever form your ten-minute conversation took, you unquestionably did transmit meaning and feelings through your facial expression, body position and proximity to the other person.

VERBAL BEHAVIOUR

Your analysis is so far only half complete, as no attention has been given to the words of your ten-minute conversation. Analysis of speech requires comprehensive rules of classification and many methods have been suggested for this. Chomsky[8] considered the problem to be one of levels. On the most obvious level is surface structure, the words themselves, where individual words symbolise specific objects or meanings. Underneath the words lies an implied meaning or 'deep structure', the ideas which form the basis of the sentence. The sentence 'Go and shut the door' suggests a surface structure of movement away, 'Go', as well as a specific action, 'shut the door'. This could be interpreted to mean 'leave, and shut the door behind you', or 'go over to the door, shut it, and then return'. The deep structure of the sentence refers to whichever one of these two (or possibly other) meanings is specifically intended.

The meaning of words is further clarified by two types of meaning, 'denotive' and 'connotive'. The words we use at the denotive level refer to types of object, e.g. building, table, or to types of experience, e.g. sound, pain. Words can also refer to kinds of situations, e.g. interview, committee meeting, or to qualities, e.g. effectiveness, leadership skills. The denotive meaning refers to the key features which distinguish a particular word. However, these key features by no means contain all the meaning a word may possess. The denotive meaning of the word 'wife' is simply a woman who is married to a man. But if you are a married man the word wife will almost certainly arouse ideas and feelings associated with your own wife; these are the connotive meaning. In everyday situations we are often only fleetingly aware, if at all, of the connotive meaning of a word, as many words give rise to a consistent connotive response on our part which makes us take the connotive meaning as the 'real' meaning of the word, while at the same time being frequently unaware of what this 'real', associative, meaning actually is. For some words the connotive meaning is particularly powerful, e.g. 'sex', and will depend on individual attitudes and experience, on how much we enjoy sex and with whom, etc. Similarly the words 'boss' and 'company' are likely to evoke your personal feelings about your boss and the company you work for.

THINKING AND FEELING

This analysis points us towards two levels of existence, 'thinking' and 'feeling', which encompass every aspect of our lives, and which are reflected in the words we use. In some situations one of these may appear to dominate, e.g. in intimate discussion with our spouse our feelings may dominate, while in planning a new salary structure for the business our thinking may dominate. Most situations we experience involve a mixture of both thinking and feeling. If the car will not start just as we are about to leave for work in the morning, we are likely to go through a mixture of both thinking and feeling. Our initial reaction after the car has not started at the first turn of the ignition may be to try a few more times, a clear piece of thinking and problem-solving behaviour. After a few minutes of this we may become exasperated, perhaps curse the car or kick it, an expression of our negative feelings. After this we may become worried about what our colleagues will think of us for being late for an important meeting (more feelings). After that we may decide to adjust the engine, e.g. dry the spark plugs, or check the ignition coils. This would be thinking or problem-solving behaviour.

Almost all the work situations we experience involve a mixture of problem-solving and emotional behaviour. When conducting an interview our main objective is likely to be the gathering of information about the candidate (problem-solving). However during this activity we may well experience feelings, e.g. when sharing a joke with the candidate, or becoming aware of our personal liking or otherwise for him or her. Similarly when conducting a departmental meeting we may be attempting to tackle some complex problem but will experience feelings which we will share with our colleagues, e.g. our satisfaction that we are making progress, or annoyance at a belligerent colleague, or an expression of appreciation to a co-worker who has put forward a particularly constructive suggestion. While in theory it is often considered inappropriate to express feelings at work, we do so consistently. In many instances our feelings will be communicated less by words than non-verbally by our facial expressions, body posture, and spatial relations with others.

Returning to the ten-minute conversation you recalled, it would be interesting to divide the contents of what was said in terms of thinking and feeling. Did the conversation contain mainly an exchange of factual information, or did you use words such as I feel, I like, it makes me so angry, I'm worried, you don't understand, rubbish, do it properly next time? Such words express feelings and emotions. Most likely your conversation contained a mixture of factual information and feelings. Try to recall its content.

By recalling the verbal and non-verbal communications of your conversation you will have undertaken a much more thorough analysis of both your own and the other person's behaviour than you probably do normally. You may have found that the non-verbal communication expressed somewhat different things than the words themselves, or that they were complementary and compatible. Once a conversation is concluded we tend only to recall the main outcome, and as a rule we do not go over it and attempt to identify specific things that were expressed with and without words. As a result of this process you will have started to use Behaviour Technology. You will have brought into focus the facts of what you and the other person communicated during your conversation. In some areas your recall will not have been perfect, and in other parts your perception may differ from what the other person believes occurred during the conversation. Nevertheless a substantial part of what you recalled will certainly have been correct.

If an employee fails to achieve a satisfactory level of performance, we rarely examine all the facts about what the employee has been doing which is leading to poor performance. Often we arrive at conclusions without considering the facts in anything like the detail you just used to analyse your ten-minute conversation. How frequently do you or your colleagues actively consider the non-verbal communications of an employee, the direct expression of feelings, as well as the evidence of problem-solving?

Behaviour Technology has as its objective the solving of human problems based on use of behaviour data. In common with other technologies, e.g. microchip technology, mechanical engineering and structural engineering, Behaviour Technology uses the available data about a problem in order to solve it. Until recently the bulk of applied behavioural science has to a great extent ignored the facts of what people do, and concentrated instead on elegant academic theories. In this way managers have been diverted from the core requirements when trying to improve employee performance; namely identifying the facts of what employees are doing.

ORIGINS OF BEHAVIOUR TECHNOLOGY

Behaviour Technology has already been adopted to solve some organisational problems. The first important development took place during the Second World War in both the British and German armies' officer selection procedures. The problem both armies faced was to identify young men from the ranks who had the most likely chance of making a success of an officer's role. The depletion of manpower brought about by death in battle created a shortfall of trained manpower to move into more senior jobs. To overcome the problem both sides designed selection procedures, which have since become known as assessment centres. These attempted to predict individual ability to perform a job for which the candidate had had no formal experience. Assessment involved a simulation of the job of an officer in a series of structured tasks over a few days. Candidates were assessed on these tasks against the behaviour and performance which were considered most essential for success as an officer. Since the war, assessment centres have come to be used increasingly in the United States, and are now gradually becoming used in other industrialised countries.

The unique feature of assessment centres compared to other selection methods is that they involve systematic assessment of the actual behaviour and performance of the candidate. Other assessment devices, such as interviews, rely on reported behaviour, while psychological tests rely on indirect assessment, mostly on the basis of pencil and paper questionnaires. An assessment centre involves candidates tackling a series of tasks or problem situations which have been carefully constructed to resemble or simulate the job for which they are being assessed. Trained assessors observe and record the behaviour and performance of candidates tackling these tasks. Only after the exercise is the record of the candidate's performance and behaviour evaluated. A more detailed description of assessment centres is given in Chapter 9.

The other major area where Behaviour Technology has been applied is in interpersonal skill training. Management training in skills such as leadership, and consulting traditionally relied on lectures about theories of leadership, influence and motivation. Over the last decade a significant shift has occurred in many organisations sponsoring such courses. Instead of merely providing trainees with a mass of ideas, training time involves providing direct feedback to trainees about their own performance in tackling the designated tasks. For example courses in selection interviewing now give candidates a chance to conduct a live interview, and then receive feedback on their performance. This type of training is usually referred to as experiential, as candidates learn from their own experiences. Such training is now commonly used to develop skills in public speaking, interviewing, leadership and working with groups. Interpersonal skill training will be considered in more detail in a later chapter.

Behaviour Technology differs from conventional methods and approaches in the applied behavioural sciences. In place of elegant models and theories about why people behave in particular ways, BT emphasises the need to collect objective information about the way they actually do behave. By collecting solid evidence about what a person is doing we can make accurate assessments and interpretations about the factors which determine this, and then plan actions which will bring about the desired changes. In the same way that other technologies develop through practical experience of problem-solving, so also can Behaviour Technology.

REFERENCES

1) Freud, S., *Two Short Accounts of Psychoanalysis*, Penguin, 1962.
2) Blake, R.R. and Mouton, J.S., *The Managerial Grid*, Gulf, 1964.
3) Fiedler, F., 'Validation and Extension of the Contingency Model of Leadership Effectiveness', *Psychological Bulletin*, 1971, 76, 128–48.
4) Reddin, *Managerial Effectiveness*, McGraw Hill, 1970.
5) Fast, J., *Body Language*, Souvenir Press, 1971.
6) Osgood, C.E., 'Dimensionality of the Semantic Space for Communication via Facial Aggression', *Scandinavian Journal of Psychology*, 7: 1–30.
7) Hall, E.T., *The Silent Language*, Doubleday, 1959.
8) Chomsky, N., *Language and Mind*, Harcourt Brace Jovanovich, 1968.

2 Defining behaviour and performance

The greatest difficulty in applying Behaviour Technology is to find a simple language to describe behaviour, and this chapter addresses that issue. For the language to be of practical value it must be applicable not only to assessment centre situations, but to any business relationship, e.g. negotiations with customers and trade union officials, department meetings, and day to day boss—subordinate discussions. The framework should be equally applicable to line managers, salesmen, accountants and development engineers. It also should be capable of describing the emotions expressed between people, and the different behaviours people use to solve problems. In short, the language must be applicable to any situation or relationship encountered in an organisation. The language we select for our application of Behaviour Technology should meet the following criteria:

(a) *Relationship adaptability*. The framework should be usuable in any individual or group relationship, whatever the previous experience of the parties (including those where conflict, co-operation or no previous relationship may exist).

(b) *Role application*. The framework should be applicable to any level or job role in an organisation, ranging from the shop floor to the board room, irrespective of function, industry or size of business. The language must be able to cope with a variety of objectives, including those where there is no common or shared objective.

(c) *Describe feelings*. The language will be required to describe behaviour which expresses feelings, both positive and negative, including joy, superiority, anger, acquiescence, etc.

(d) *Describe problem-solving*. The framework should be able to handle a diverse range of problem-solving behaviours encountered in business situations. Because this book deals with management it will refer to cerebral as opposed to physical problem-solving.

(e) *Reliability of classification*. So that managers can discuss and use behaviour data in a meaningful way, the labels used to describe any piece of behaviour must be clearly discernible to anyone who understands the classification system. The acid test of this would be that different observers of the same piece of behaviour would label it in the same way.

(f) *Ease of use.* If the language used to describe behaviour is to have any practical value it must be relatively easy to learn and use. It should not require years of training, but be within the grasp of the average line manager within a short period of training.

Providing a language for describing behaviour which meets these criteria is no easy matter. However, if the language fails to meet them it would have little value in solving organisation problems. The need of the manager is for a vehicle he or she can use to tackle all human resource problems.

Other technologies have their own well established languages and concepts for tackling problems. The computer specialist has at his disposal many terms to describe the subject with which he is involved. Terms such as random access, distributed processing, disc packs, and transaction processing all denote precise aspects of computer technology. If a line manager wishes to tackle a computing problem he has no alternative but to understand the relevant concepts which are involved in the problem he is trying to solve.

Similarly if a manager wishes to set up a new production plant he will need to come to grips with factors such as batch sizes, product variations, inventory levels, lead times for bought in components, etc. These are not vague ill-defined notions, but rather definite concepts which are of critical importance when setting up a new manufacturing facility. Obviously top management will not require the same degree of detailed understanding as the production engineer, but they will need to have a grasp of some of these factors if they are to do more than merely rubber stamp the proposals put forward by a manufacturing specialist.

While the manager of the sales department may not need to understand anything about computers (although he increasingly does), he will need to know about working with people. The finance director equally may not need to know much about computer-controlled machine tools, apart from the fact that they achieve the required return on capital employed. He or she will, however, need to know about working with people.

One common concern shared by all managers is working with people and solving human problems. It does not matter whether the manager is in charge of three thousand or three subordinates, has a budget of £500 millions or £50,000, he will encounter human resource problems simply through working with other people. So managers, irrespective of their function in a business, need a language they can use to tackle these. This chapter describes such a language.

Two separate languages will be used: Transactional Analysis and the Problem-Solving Dimensions. These respectively classify behaviour which expresses feelings, and rational problem-solving behaviour. Together the two provide a comprehensive and adaptable framework which can be used by managers to understand the actions of others. These frameworks are considered in the context of other frameworks for evaluating behaviour in specific problem situations in the chapters in Part Two.

Integrating Transactional Analysis and the Problem-Solving Dimensions provides a comprehensive language for categorising all possible forms of behaviour. They provide an unique opportunity for Behaviour Technology to become a truly practical tool for management: a technology for solving human problems. The validity of the approach is further enhanced by its potential in everyday non-work situations in our personal lives.

TRANSACTIONAL ANALYSIS

Transactional Analysis is a framework for understanding what people do, and particularly the variety of feelings they express. It was founded by Eric Berne,[1] an American psychiatrist who sought a language for use in helping his patients understand themselves. In contrast to the traditional language of psychology, which is incomprehensible to most of us (including many psychologists), Eric Berne developed Transactional Analysis so that everyone could better understand and describe behaviour. It is concerned with what people do, rather than abstract ideas. Communication and behaviour were viewed by Berne as a series of exchanges or transactions between people. If I meet you and say 'hello' and you nod your head and smile back at me, we have exchanged greetings; there has been a behaviour transaction between us. Transactional Analysis, or TA, is the analysis of transactions between people.

The framework of behaviour which makes up transactions is based on the 'ego states'. These are three distinct and seperate observable behaviour patterns which reflect states of being. We all use all three 'ego states' to varying degrees, and can observe changes from one to the other through distinct changes in facial expression, vocabulary, gesture and posture. The manager who frowns when he is interrupted in a meeting when the phone goes is exhibiting certain ego state behaviours, as is the supervisor who responds to the production plan of the manufacturing director by asking 'What are the time scales for getting this done?' The salesmen who winks at the attractive secretary passing him in the corridor is in a third ego state. The behaviour of these three people is respectively described as 'Parent' 'Adult' and 'Child' ego states. At any one moment we are in one of the ego states, but have the capacity to switch quickly from one to the other, and indeed we do so frequently.

THE PARENT EGO STATE

The Parent ego state refers to rules, admonitions, and beliefs. These can be expressed as critical and demanding (as in the above example of the manager who frowned), or concerned and sympathetic. The 'Critical Parent' sets limits and makes judgements. Phrases such as 'Never turn the machine on without checking the drill turret first,' or 'You must get this report finished by tonight,' or 'Don't question my orders — just get on with it,' are typical Parent statements. Words such as 'never', 'must', 'always' suggest the Parent ego state. Non-verbal communication which suggests that someone is in a Critical Parent ego state are a furrowed brow, pointed finger, head tilted up and peering down, and a scowling expression.

The sympathetic or 'Nurturing Parent' is also expressing judgements and beliefs with phrases such as 'Let me know if you get stuck and want help,' 'Don't worry, I'll sort it out for you.' Typical non-verbal behaviours which characterise the Nurturing Parent are the pat on the back, the benevolent smile. As with the other ego states, the Parent can be used in a variety of situations, both positively and negatively. We might tell our subordinate 'You must get the report ready on time for the marketing director before he goes abroad.' This has a positive message in terms of achieving results according to timescales, and is an example of constructive use of the Parent ego state for business success. Equally, use of the Nurturing Parent in a conversation to a new colleague who has just started work in our organisation may be appropriate — 'This is a confusing organisation to work in — if there is anything you are not sure about come and ask me.'

Much of our Parent ego state behaviour originates from when we were very small and were told what to do and what not to do by our mother and father. As we got older and moved to groups outside our family, and joined organisations such as schools and business companies, we took on some of their values, judgements and beliefs as part of our own Parent ego state. The organisation in which you work will have certain rules about how to dress, how you can speak to superiors, and the extent to which you should be punctual, even though many of these are not written down. To what extent have you adopted these rules about dress in your behaviour? Do you wear the same clothes as everyone else, or are you an individualist who dresses either much more formally or more casually than your colleagues? You will have your own standards and rules about time-keeping, the format of a good report, what makes a fair day's work, and many other things. Your views on these are the internal rules you have for yourself, and which you will express in your behaviour towards others.

THE ADULT EGO STATE

The Adult ego state is made up of rational, logical and analytical behaviour. It is based on our objective experiences and exploration of the environment and develops throughout our life. Typical Adult statements might be: 'What time is it?' 'Why did the machine break down?' 'The statistics suggest that . . .,' 'The cost of launching the new product will be . . .'. Adult ego state behaviour selects data, works things out, evaluates alternatives, and estimates probability. The Adult ego state operates like a computer, and is a much more complex computer than any that man has yet made. As such the Adult is void of emotion and is dominated by rationality and logic. This is emphasised by the typical non-verbal behaviour of someone in their Adult ego state. When we are in our Adult ego state we usually have a straight back, level eye contact and are aware and attentive to what is going on around us. Such phrases as 'has his feet on the ground' or 'level-headed' precisely describe the Adult non-verbal behaviour of having both feet on the ground and having a level head (as opposed to a tilted or sideways head). These phrases suggest that the person described is someone who spends a lot of time in their Adult ego state.

The Adult ego state is an essential requirement for any job. Irrespective of whether we are a shop floor operator or managing director of a multi-national corporation, we are employed to do a job of work involving problem-solving. The problems might be about scheduling maintenance, or about estimating long-term world wide oil requirements and their implications for exploration activities, but both require the use of the Adult ego state.

It is often believed that at work we spend most of our time in the Adult ego state. However, while we may spend some time analysing data, calculating, planning and other rational activities, for many of us this accounts for only part of the time we spend at work. While many business meetings have an objective, and a written agenda, a significant proportion of our time in the meeting is not spent on solving problems, or giving and receiving pure information. How often have you attended meetings and felt afterwards that it should have taken far less time? When this occurs it is because either other people's Adult ego states were functioning less well than your own, or that their and perhaps your other two ego states were used more in the meeting.

THE CHILD EGO STATE

The Child ego state expresses our feelings and responses to things either in the world outside, or within ourselves. Our Child ego state exercises a very powerful control over our lives, and is the source of energy and happiness. If we are eager to get on with a new project, or feel bored about the whole thing, this is due to the feelings in our Child ego state. The feelings can be spontaneous and expressive as in the 'Free Child', or they may be compliant as in the 'Adapted Child'.

The Free Child represents the way we were when we were born, is self-centred, and operates without regard for other people, groups or organisations. It is carefree and expresses what we want directly with words such as 'I want' 'I feel fantastic', 'Ow'. Typical non-verbal behaviour would be laughing, loud talking, relaxed asymmetrical posture, cuddling, sobbing, fists clenched. The Free Child provides charm and warmth in our lives, and is the source of fun.

Our memories of school and our first job will have taught us that life in an organisation requires adherence to certain rules and standards of conduct if we are to continue as a member of that organisation. We were praised for doing the 'right things' and sticking to the rules, and punished when we broke the rules. At school we were taught to attend lessons (even when we may have preferred to be playing in the school grounds) and to do our homework on time (even when it may have been much more fun to go to the movies). At work we almost certainly had some of those early rules from school reinforced, such as the need to be punctual. At work we also had new rules imposed on us, for instance in organisations where it is not the done thing to argue with the boss, or others where it is not the job of juniors to make suggestions for improving things because their job is to do as they are told. As a result of these rules and standards we probably made adaptations to get along with other people, and this type of behaviour is known as the 'Adapted Child'. Typical words used by the Adapted Child are 'I'll try', 'Please can I . . .' 'Excuse me, but . . .'. Such phrases are often accompanied by the non-verbal behaviour of downcast eyes, slumped and dejected posture, or vigorous head nodding.

A degree of compliance to the rules and standards of organisations is essential if we wish to remain a member, and get along with others. But we may over-adapt to the rules given to us, and this can create barriers and blockages. It is interesting to contrast those rules we adhere to as a result of messages we received from our mother and father, and those we received from the organisation we work for. An important revelation to a junior manager in his late forties at a training course was when he told others in the group 'All my life I thought that all I had to do to get promotion was to work hard. I now understand why I have not progressed in this company.' The company was one where power was exercised by a few senior individuals, and getting on was determined not so much by the quality of an employee's work as by compliance to those few people in authority. To this particular manager this awareness was an important insight into what was happening to his career.

The final part of the Child ego state is the 'Little Professor', which is about feelings of an intuitive creative kind. Moments of genius when we realise in an instant the way to solve a problem, or interrelate what were previously two separate and independent pieces of data into a coherent picture, are examples of our use of our Little Professors. The artist and research scientist rely on Little Professor behaviour to help them achieve success. While thinking and analysis assists in arriving at solutions, it is the sudden 'I've got it!' which often puts the answer before us. This seems to have occurred with many of the great thinkers who have influenced us, including Aristotle, Newton, DaVinci, and Einstein, who all relied on their Adult eto state, together with the Little Professor, to come to their profound conclusions about the world we live in.

Examples of Little Professor words are 'Gosh — I've got it,' 'Ah . . . ,' 'Brilliant!' Non-verbal behaviour includes looking wide-eyed, sudden excitement to express oneself, spontaneous movement of the body from a previously still position.

It may at first be difficult to identify the link between the three parts of the Child ego state. However, this becomes clearer when we recognise that the Natural Child, Adapted Child and Little Professor are all concerned with the expression of feelings. Your feelings, as you know from experience, can take many forms, and TA classifies feelings overall as being spontaneous, compliant to rules, or of a creative type. This contrasts with the Adult ego state which is void of emotion, and the Parent which is concerned with making judgements and evaluations of people and things.

The words 'Parent', 'Adult' and 'Child' used from a TA point of view have different meanings from those used in normal conversation. Interestingly, though, this choice of words is based on their significance in the everyday world. Grown-ups with children spend a lot of their time telling them what they should and should not do; the Parent ego state. Grown-ups together at work do spend time solving problems which concern them, and exhibit the Adult ego state. Children express their feelings as a rule much more readily than grown-ups, and joy, excitement, compliance and creativity can very readily be detected when we observe children playing. When we talk about a grown-up being in the Child ego state we do not mean that they are behaving in a childish or immature fashion, but that their behaviour expresses feelings.

The ego states provide a comprehensive framework in which we can classify what people do. At any moment we are in one of the ego states, and this applies now to you as reader of this book. If you are thinking that what you have read is a load of rubbish, you are most probably in the Parent ego state. If you are reading this attentively, evaluating what has been said so far and comparing it to what you already know about psychology, you are almost certainly in the Adult ego state. However, should your reaction be one of great enthusiasm, anger, or total agreement with everything that has been said, then you are likely to be in one part of the Child ego state. You may want to consider your posture and body position as an indicator of your ego state. Does it match the ego state you think you are in?

TRANSACTIONS

When two people communicate or engage in a transaction this involves
behaviour from one of the ego states. Thus if a colleague telephones you
and asks 'Did you take delivery of the new word processor?' and you reply
'Yes, it arrived this morning,' you have engaged in a conversation between
your Adult and your colleague's Adult. We can visualise transactions
between people as lines going between two sets of three circles, each set of
three circles representing the three ego states, as in Figure 2.1. A transaction occurs when person X in the diagram communicates with person Y
by giving a stimulus from one of his ego state to one of the ego states of
person Y, and person Y responds from one of his ego states to an ego state
of person X.

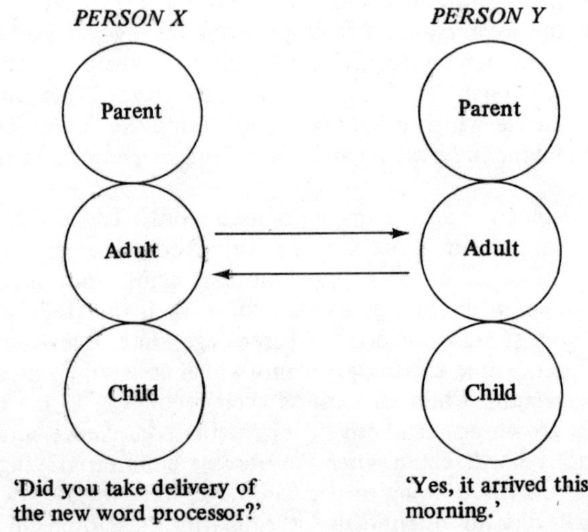

Figure 2.1   Adult to Adult Transactions

When communication occurs to and from the same ego state, as in the
example above concerning the word processor, we say it is a parallel transaction. Quite simply the lines between the two sets of circles are parallel,
as shown in the diagram. Parallels, or 'complementary transactions' as they
may be called, can occur between one person's Adult and the Adult of
another person (as in our original example), or between the Parent of one
and the Parent of the other, or between the Child of two people. A typical
Parent to Parent type of conversation might go something like:

Peter: The trouble with the trade union is they never understand that we
   have a business to run.

John: Yes, they're stupid, every year they put in an outrageous wage demand.

Typically parallel Parent to Parent conversations, as depicted in Figure 2.2, involve complaining about someone else — it could be the union, senior management, the suppliers, the customers, etc. Child to Child transactions involve the expression of feelings, as in a conversation between a boy and a girl who are saying goodnight after meeting at a party:

Anne: It's been a wonderful evening.
Tom: I've really enjoyed being with you, I'd like to see you again.

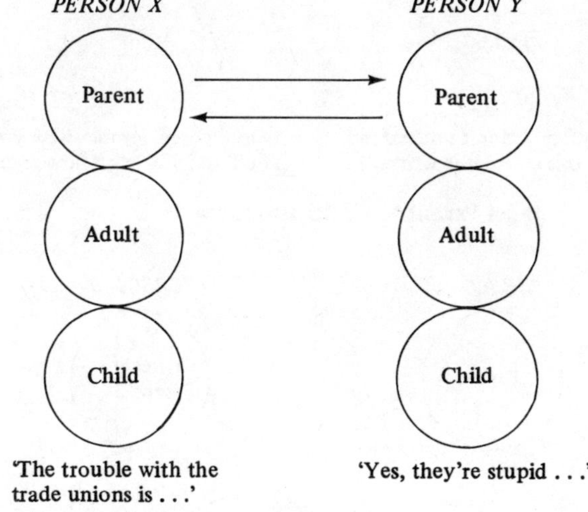

Figure 2.2   Parent to Parent Transactions

Child to Child transactions can involve the expression of negative feelings, as happens when we quarrel and let the other person know how furious we are with them.

Another type of parallel transaction occurs between the Parent in one person and the Child in another, as in Figure 2.3. Such a conversation might take the form of:

Secretary: I give up. I don't understand how this calculator works.
Boss: Don't worry, let me show you. You'll quickly learn to use it.

In this case the secretary is using her Adapted Child in criticising herself, and the boss is using his Nurturing Parent to encourage her.

So long as both people remain in the same ego states, parallel transactions can go on continuously and smoothly. However, an unexpected

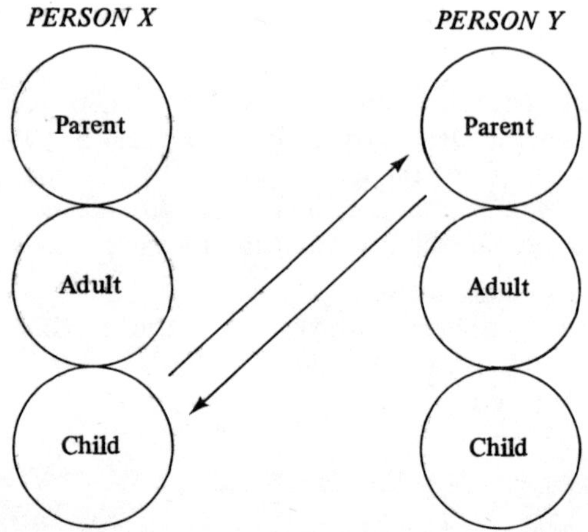

Figure 2.3   Parallel Parent to Child Transactions

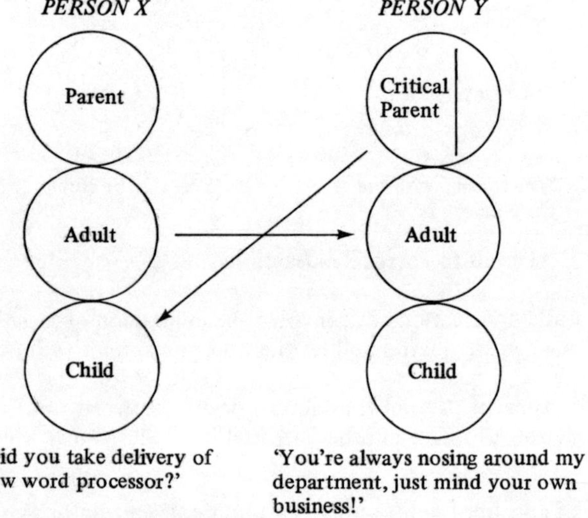

Figure 2.4   Crossed Transactions

response may occur to a stimulus and the lines on the diagram may cross
(Figure 2.4), leading to a blockage of communication. An example of this
may occur if the colleague had responded differently to the question 'Did

you take delivery of the new word processor?' (Adult to Adult) with 'You're always nosing around my department, just mind your own business' (Critical Parent to Adapted Child). Another common type of crossed transaction occurs when two people blame each other, when a row develops:

Roger: You never get your monthly report in on time, it's just not good
    enough.
Nigel: You always expect me to achieve miracles — you'll just have to let
    me get on with the job my own way.

In this case the stimulus is from each person's Critical Parent to the other's Adapted Child, as shown in Figure 2.5.

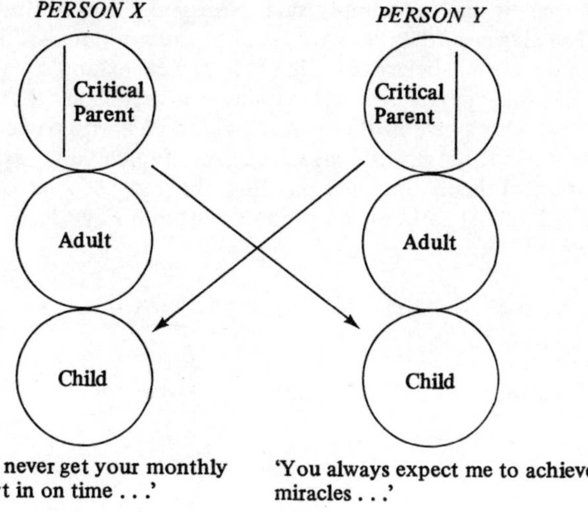

Figure 2.5   Crossed Transactions

When we get involved in crossed transactions we stop communicating smoothly, and one of the people concerned will need to change their ego state if they want to continue to relate. A good indication of a crossed transaction is when we say something to someone and they respond in an unexpected way and we get a sudden lump in our throat.

The third type of communication is the ulterior transaction. Ulterior transactions involve one person sending messages simultaneously to two separate ego states in another. One example might be when a boss says to a subordinate who has arrived late for work 'What time did you arrive in the office?' On the surface this could be seen as an Adult to Adult transaction; however, in the context this is only part of the message. Underneath it implies a Critical Parent to Child message at the psychological level — 'You should not have arrived late at work.' We often use ulterior transactions when we want to convey messages in a disguised and socially acceptable way. The classic example is the cliché of boy to girl:

Boy: Do you want to come up and see my etchings?
Girl: Yes, that would be interesting.

Once again the words are literally Adult to Adult, but underneath the psychological message is 'I'd like to be alone with you,' and the response is 'That would be fun,' — Child to Child transactions (Figure 2.6). We frequently use ulterior transactions to save face and avoid rejection. If the boy had said outright 'I'd like to be alone with you,' he might have risked the possible response from the girl 'Don't be disgusting,' which is more of a rejection than if she had simply said 'No thanks, I'm not interested in etchings.' The giveaway that we are engaging in ulterior transactions comes from our non-verbal behaviour. In the earlier example of the boss addressing the subordinate who arrives late, it is very likely that the words 'What time did you arrive in the office?' would be accompanied by hands on hips, furrowed brow, or pursed lips, all typical non-verbal Parent communication. Equally the boy inviting the girl to come and see his etchings would almost certainly have had a glint in his eyes!

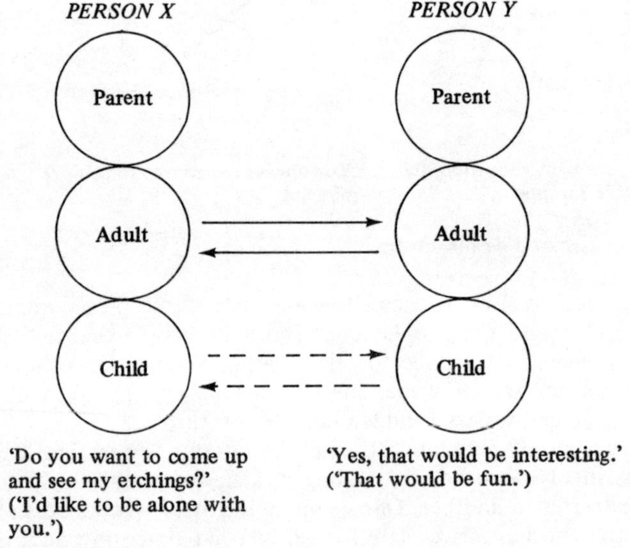

Figure 2.6   Ulterior Transactions

STROKES

Having used Transactional Analysis to understand how we communicate with others we now can consider the question of why we do so. According to TA the reason we communicate with people is to obtain 'Strokes'. Strokes are any act which implies recognition of another person, and can range from the casual nod of the head to a colleague we pass in the corridor, to the passionate embrace of lovers. Strokes, both verbal and physical, are considered to be the single most important motivator in our lives.

The physical intimacy we experienced as babies in the arms of our mother was the most basic and intimate recognition most of us ever received, and quite literally involved our receiving strokes. As we grew up we replaced much of the close physical relationship with our mother with non-physical symbolic forms of recognition. We receive a mild stroke when a colleague greets us with 'Good morning', and a more powerful stroke when the boss tells us 'It's really good to have you in my department,' or 'That was an outstanding piece of work you did.' Most of the strokes we give and receive at work are verbal, and meet the basic need all of us have to be recognised.

Each of us has our personal preferences for the types of strokes we most want to receive. Some employees may want to have their Adult ego state flattered by being told how good their work is. Other employees may want to be liked as a person, rather than for what they do, and this would involve them in trying to get their Child stroked. Yet others want to get their Nurturing Parent stroked by having others coming to them with their problems, so that they can help and nurture them. All of us have our preferred stroke patterns, and these determine the ways in which we communicate with others, and the types of people we prefer to communicate with.

Strokes, like food, are a basic requirement for survival. Spitz[2] pointed out that when deprived of sufficient stimulation through touch a baby will degenerate physically as well as psychologically. The work of psychologists who have studied institutionalised children, such as Bowlby,[3] lend considerable weight to this conclusion, as do the laboratory studies of monkeys which were reared without their mothers.[4] In the grown-up world we mostly survive to obtain strokes from others which resemble those we received as a small infant.

Our desire for strokes is so strong that we prefer to receive negative strokes rather than no strokes at all. Children will prefer to be told off or scolded rather than be totally ignored, and this explains why children may misbehave, apparently without reason. If a child's parents are not paying it attention, the child will force them to pay attention by doing something which is considered very naughty, just to get mother's or father's attention. Constant repetition of this type of stroke pattern can ultimately lead to being conditioned that the only way one can receive strokes is to misbehave. Occasionally we come across employees who appear consistently to break the rules, even though these have been carefully and painstakingly explained to them. In such cases the employee may simply be repeating the pattern they got into as an infant of obtaining negative strokes.

As a result of conditioning during our childhood most of us attempt to repeat later on in life the stroke pattern we received then. This is known as the 'stroke balance', and we feel most comfortable when this is maintained. When we receive either too many or too few strokes of either a positive or a negative kind than we expect from our preferred stroke balance, we set up situations which redress the balance. Sometimes if an employee has not received sufficient positive Adult strokes for his work he will work particularly hard to get these from the boss. Other people may seek to keep up the balance of negative strokes they receive, and commit absolute howlers every now and again just to receive their share of negative strokes. Having once been reprimanded for the howler, the employee will have restored his balance of negative strokes, and again continue to perform satisfactorily. Do you know anyone like that?

People who use their Child ego state a lot in transactions tend to want to receive a lot of strokes for being themselves, while those who use mainly the Adult ego state will seek strokes for what they do. In contrast those who predominantly use Parent ego state behaviour will want to obtain strokes from others who feel grateful to them (Adapted Child), or will obtain strokes by making others feel bad (Critical Parent).

GAMES

Games are the final aspect of Transactional Analysis to be considered here. A game, as described by Eric Berne[5], involves a series of predictable transactions which result in at least one of the players receiving negative strokes and feeling bad.

Games are destructive transactions. They avoid understanding between people, and prevent them from getting on with real work. We frequently play games while believing we are actually engaged in work; however, the sudden feeling of 'ugh' or 'here we go again' when we are on the receiving end of a game demonstrates that the psychological 'pay-off' has occurred. Games are a repetitive form of transaction, and we tend to play the same ones with specific people.

There are many different types of games, and most of us have one or two which we prefer playing. One common game is when we are asked for advice on how to overcome a problem, and every suggestion we put forward is unacceptable. This game is called 'Yes but' and its real objective is for the person who asked for advice to be able to give negative strokes to the person who makes suggestions by telling them that all their suggestions are a waste of time. Some senior managers are especially fond of playing this with subordinates, as are line managers who call on staff advisors (including personnel). An example might be:

Line manager: What shall I do about Smith? He really is not performing satisfactorily.

Personnel manager: Did you raise the problem in the performance appraisal discussion you had with him two weeks ago?

Line manager: Of course not, appraisal is all a waste of time – we only do it to keep you people in personnel happy.

Personnel manager: You could call him into your office and discuss the problem with him, and tell him he must improve.

Line manager: I can't do that, he's a member of the union, and will claim that I threatened him.

Personnel manager: If you like I could be present when you call him in, and be a witness to what you said.

Line manager: No, this is a personal thing between him and me, and I don't want anyone else present.

Personnel manager: You could use the disciplinary procedure, and write him a formal memo, which puts the problem in black and white.

Line manager: These are all useless suggestions – I don't have the time to go in for all this fancy footwork. You personnel people are all the same, you put forward ideas which are bureaucratic and time wasting. I really don't know why we employ people in personnel.

Does this pattern of transactions sound familiar?

In games there are one of three positions the players can adopt: Persecutor, Rescuer or Victim. In the above example the line manager starts off as Victim (he has a difficult problem to solve with Smith), and the personnel manager takes on the role of Rescuer (he puts forward suggestions on how to sort out Smith). The roles change in the final part, and the line manager takes on the role of Persecutor (telling the personnel manager that he is useless and giving him negative strokes), while the personnel manager takes on the role of Victim (being told that he is worthless).

Subordinates are just as likely to initiate games with their bosses as the other way round, and games are played in private life as much as (or even more than) in work situations. Most families have their own favourite games, which are played as part of the round of family life. Whatever games we play, whether at home or at work, they serve as a powerful source of reinforcement for our preferred ego states. If we have a large Critical Parent we are likely to engage in games which end up with us as

Persecutor in the punch line. If we have a large Adapted Child we are likely to play games which lead to our ending up in the Victim position. Alternatively if we have a large Nurturing Parent we will prefer to play games in which we end up as Rescuer.

Table 2.1 summarises some of the games commonly found in organisations.

Table 2.1

SOME COMMON ORGANISATION GAMES

Game title	Typical starting behaviour of game initiator	Game payoff for initiator	Game result for other player
'Yes But'	'Help me solve this problem . . .'	Persecutor Role – any suggestion the other makes is useless	Victim Role – Any suggestions are worthless
'Kick Me'	'I've made another mistake . . .'	Victim Role – 'I deserve to be reprimanded'	Persecutor Role – 'You never get anything right'
'Harried'	'I'll take on every problem that needs fixing'	Victim Role – 'I can't cope with all the work – I work weekends/ have an ulcer from the strain'	No other player required
'Rapo'	Sexual 'come on' – verbal or non-verbal cue for a sexual advance	Persecutor Role – when the other responds they are given brush off, put down for sticking their neck out	Victim Role – feels bad for responding to 'come on'
'Blemish'	'This piece of work must be 100% perfect'	Persecutor Role – can and does always find some fault with the other's work	Victim Role – feels bad that they can never get things right
'Now I've Got You, You Son of a Bitch'	'Now will you do the following' (which cannot be done)	Persecutor Role – lets the other know they are incompetent and inadequate	Victim Role – has really made a mess of the task
'Ain't It Awful'	'Things are really bad round here . . .'	Victim Role – 'Nothing ever goes right, despite my efforts'	Rescuer Role – feels sympathy for misery of other person

Game title	Typical starting behaviour of game initiator	Game payoff for initiator	Game result for other player
'Cornered'	'Now you just get on with solving this problem' (and I won't tell the ground-rules)	Persecutor Role – lets others set themselves up – by not giving guidance	Victim Role – has really failed to do a good job
'Uproar'	Attacks other person aggressively to provoke a hostile reaction from them.	Persecutor Role – sets up angry exchanges, which prevent under-standing and parallel transaction. Also avoids work.	Victim Role – defensive reation to being persecuted.

PROBLEM-SOLVING DIMENSIONS

While Transactional Analysis provides a comprehensive vehicle for classifying behaviour which expresses feelings and emotions, it provides only a single category for classifying problem-solving behaviours; the Adult ego state. Although this may be sufficient for some requirements, it is insufficient for management purposes, where a wide range of problem-solving behaviours are required. While a manager's success will obviously depend to a large extent on his or her ability to relate to others, it will also depend on his or her possession of problem-solving skills related to the job being performed. In some jobs the relationship skills may be more important than the problem-solving skills, while in other jobs the reverse may be the case. One fact that can be stated with certainty is that every management job requires behavioural skills in both areas. In many research laboratories particularly high levels of problem-solving skills are required from employees. While relationship skills may be less important, it is nevertheless essential that a research scientist, however brilliant at problem-solving, can relate to his colleagues. In contrast the relationship skills of many salesmen are frequently regarded as their dominant strength. Nevertheless without some problem-solving skills the salesman will not be able to find solutions to customers' difficulties.

The method of classifying problem-solving behaviours proposed here is based on the Development Dimension International (DDI) categories developed by Dr William Byham.[6] These consist of over forty types of problem-solving behaviours, each of which has been precisely defined. Many of these behaviours can be thought of as a subdivision of the Adult ego state. In this way the two frameworks of Transactional Analysis and Problem-Solving Dimensions can be seen as complementary, rather than in any way in opposition to one another.

For practical purposes the forty problem-solving behaviours described by DDI will rarely if ever be used together. From my own experience some fifteen of these will be relevant to most organisations. For any one job some of these problem-solving behaviours are likely to be particularly salient. In practice, therefore, when we categorise a particular manager's or group of managers' behaviours we are likely only to need to refer to some of the dimensions. The most commonly used problem-solving behaviours are shown in Table 2.2.

Our total range of problem-solving behaviours will often encompass an element of many other behaviours. However, only some of these will be of critical importance.

Table 2.2

MAJOR PROBLEM-SOLVING DIMENSIONS

Problem analysis. Identifying problems, seeking relevant information, recognising important information and identifying possible causes of problems. Examples are:
(a) Seeking out data from different sources as to the causes and effect of problems;
(b) Being able to see all points of view and weigh them up accordingly;
(c) Develop and consider alternative solutions to problems.

Attention to detail. Thorough approach to a task through concern for all the areas involved, no matter how small. Examples are:
(a) Taking account of detailed quantitative information on a problem, as well as the broader picture;
(b) Making no ommissions when analysing or implementing a solution;
(c) Concern for the detailed interaction of technical, administrative and human aspects of a problem.

Decisiveness. Crispness and firmness in forming judgements and making decisions for action. Examples are:
(a) Not sitting on the fence or deferring decisions unnecessarily;
(b) Clear understanding of own objectives and priorities and knowing what needs to be done;
(c) Stating decisions and proposals clearly and unambiguously.

Judgement. Standing back from a problem situation, evaluating information and settling on courses of action which are logical and rational. Examples are:
(a) Making decisions which are in the best interests of the organisation;

(b) Not allowing personal preferences, likes or dislikes to influence judge-
     ments unduly;
(c) Giving clear reasons for making decisions.

Flexibility/Adaptability. Modifying behaviour in the light of new information or changed circumstances to ensure effective achievement of a
goal. Examples are:
(a) Responding quickly when new information becomes available or
     situations change;
(b) Incorporating other people's ideas and suggestions in one's work;
(c) Revising plans and approach when circumstances make impossible to
     achieve one's original goal.

Initiative. Actively influencing events rather than passively accepting
things as they are; seeing opportunities and acting on them. Examples are:
(a) Putting forward ideas, suggestions and proposals when tackling a
     problem;
(b) Getting on with resolving problems without direction;
(c) Bringing problems or information to the attention of others who are
     involved.

Risk taking. Taking or initiating action which involves a deliberate gamble
in order to gain a recognised benefit or objective; this involves weighing
the consequences of action, and calculating the extent to which the risks
are outweighed by the possible advantages. Examples are:
(a) Initiating discussion about the consequences of failure;
(b) Consideration of a wide range of alternative strategies for the achieve-
     ment of objectives;
(c) Emphasising the possible benefits of courses of action where risks are
     involved.

Stress tolerance. Stability of performance under pressure and opposition;
ability to control emotions and make controlled responses in stressful
situations. Examples are:
(a) Not giving in when opposition or difficulties appear;
(b) Responding constructively when conflict arises;
(c) Reliability in achieving objectives.

Tenacity. Staying with a problem, objective, or line of thought until the
matter is settled. Examples are:
(a) Pursuing tasks until they are completed, not letting things slide;
(b) Not shrinking from tackling problems;
(c) Achieving objectives in the timescales laid down.

Interpersonal sensitivity/listening. Accurate perception of others' needs, feelings and views; awareness of one's own impact on others; taking others' feelings into account when determining one's behaviour. Examples are:
(a) Listening and taking account of others' points of view;
(b) Demonstrating concern for others;
(c) Ability to discuss one's own relationships directly with others.

Persuasiveness/Verbal communication. Clear presentation of ideas or facts to others and ability to convince others, whether in one to one or group interactions, or formal or informal situations. Examples are:
(a) Skill in verbal expression and clarity in presentation of information, ideas or arguments;
(b) Ability to present arguments logically and in context;
(c) Ability to evoke positive responses from others.

Leadership. Developing team work and using available resources to the full in order to achieve objectives; this can apply to groups over which the individual may or may not have formal authority. Examples are:
(a) Clarifying objectives and allocating tasks to individuals;
(b) Recognising the achievements of others and developing unity and purpose in the group, department or organisation;
(c) Being invited by others to provide direction and co-ordination.

Delegation. Effective use of human resources and staff functions; knowledge of when, how and to whom to delegate. Examples are:
(a) Involving people in decisions to gain their commitment;
(b) Actively developing subordinates by delegating tasks;
(c) Full awareness of the workload of subordinates.

Planning and organising. Establishing appropriate course of action for oneself and for others in order to achieve one's aims; this may refer to strategic planning and may include the utilisation of time, resources, etc. Examples are:
(a) Setting priorities which take account of the short and long-term needs of the business;
(b) Anticipating problems and considering the consequences of one's plans on other areas;
(c) Having a reputation for getting things done and meeting deadlines.

Management control. Creating and using controls over processes, people, and tasks; this can operate in formal or advisory situations and include overall standards as well as specific activities. Examples are:
(a) Setting up information and control systems and using them effectively;

(b) Regularly monitoring plans and progress and following up any actions taken;
(c) Setting standards for performance and keeping them under review.

Written Communication. Clear expression of ideas in writing, in a form appropriate to the situation. Examples are:
(a) Clear, unambiguous written work;
(b) Concise presentation of ideas, arguments and information;
(c) Use of language and style appropriate to the context and intended recipients.

Using the Problem-Solving Dimensions it is possible to specify the types and quantities of problem-solving behaviours used by particular individuals, as well as those required by different jobs. While writing this book I was aware that I needed to concentrate on creativity, problem analysis, attention to detail, planning and organising, and written communication. I also required high levels of tenacity in view of the other options that were available for the use of my time.

In contrast to this I am aware of needing to use other problem-solving behaviours in my job. While the amount of creativity needed is considerably less, the amount of planning and organising required is much larger. Other skills such as decisiveness and persuasiveness are required to a greater degree in my full-time job than in my writing. On the other hand, when driving a car in a hectic town centre it is necessary to exhibit high levels of flexibility/adaptability, stress tolerance, and planning.

Any given problem requires specific behaviour if it is to be tackled successfully. The value of the Problem-Solving Dimensions (PSDs) is that they can describe the precise work behaviours of an individual or group. Instead of merely specifying the tasks to be carried out, the PSDs provide a analysis of the specific behaviours required to tackle them. The role of many salesmen for example requires high levels of initiative, persuasiveness, sensitivity and tenacity. In contrast the job of a production manager may require high levels of leadership, delegation, problem analysis, judgement and decisiveness. It may be a disadvantage for a production manager to show high levels of sensitivity in his behaviour as this may detract from the performance of his job. Application of the PSDs to job analysis will be covered in detail in Chapter 4.

Even with our rigorous definitions of the PSDs it will be apparent that they can exist in different degrees. While a particular skill level of planning and organising may meet the requirements for a recent graduate joining a production department, it may not be sufficient for success in the job of a company president or chief executive. Consequently, an assessment of the Problem-Solving Dimensions will be influenced by the situation in which they occur. While a degree of planning and organising is beneficial when we go to the supermarket, this will hardly meet the level required to fulfil the role of a production planning manager, whose inventory constraints are rather more complex than the size of the deep freeze! Similarly the degree of problem analysis required to fix the fuse of an electric plug is vastly different from that required to fix a breakdown in the central processor of a large mainframe computer.

Used together with Transactional Analysis the Problem-Solving Dimensions provide a detailed and comprehensive framework for categorising and describing people's behaviour. This can be used as much in the office as in the factory. If the behaviour exhibited is predominantly concerned with expressing feelings and emotions, then TA provides the most appropriate vehicle. If the behaviour involves solving problems, the Problem-Solving Dimensions can mainly be used. In practice we are likely to encounter behaviour which contains a mixture of both problem-solving and expression of feelings. Because human behaviour is so varied and diverse we need a framework which pays attention to both facets. It is precisely because so much effort has been directed exclusively at one or the other that managers concerned with solving human resource problems have found the offerings of behavioural science unsatisfactory. The following chapter will demonstrate how TA and the PSDs can be used together to analyse actual behaviour.

REFERENCES

1) Berne, E., *What Do You Say after You Say Hello?*, Deutsch, 1974.
2) Spitz, R., 'Hospitalism: Genesis of Psychiatric Conditions in Early Childhood', *Psychological Study of the Child*, 1945, 1, 53–74.
3) Bowlby, J., *Child Care and the Growth of Love*, Penguin, 1953.
4) Harlow, H., 'Love in Infant Monkeys', *Scientific American*, June 1959.
5) Berne, E., *Games People Play*, Deutsch, 1966.
6) © Copyright 1975, Development Dimensions International, Pittsburgh, Pennsylvania, USA.

3 Applying the Behaviour Technology framework

The previous chapter described the Behaviour Technology method of categorising behaviour. This will now be used to help us better understand and evaluate communication and behaviour. While the chapters in Part Two apply Behaviour Technology to specific organisational situations, this chapter will undertake an analysis of a passage taken from a novel. This analysis is intended to show how communication and relationships can be better understood, and then made more effective, with Behaviour Technology. The author of the novel from which this passage is taken is presumed not to have been writing with Behaviour Technology in mind!

You are invited to analyse the TA ego states and Problem-Solving Dimensions which appear in the behaviour of individuals in this passage. After making your own interpretation, compare this to the analysis provided later in the chapter.

FROM ARTHUR HAILEY, *THE MONEY CHANGERS*[1]

The passage below describes part of a board meeting of the First Mercantile American Bank concerning a proposed loan to the Supranational Company.

> Disregarding the growing hostility, Alex ploughed on, 'Other aspects of the Supranational loan disturb me equally. To make the money available we're to cut mortgage lending and small loans. In these two areas alone the bank will be defective in its public service.'
>
> Jerome Patterton said huffily, 'It's been clearly stated that those cutbacks are temporary.'
>
> 'Yes,' Alex acknowledged, 'Except no one will say just how temporary, or what happens to the business and good will the bank will lose while the ban is on. And then there's the third area of cutback which we haven't touched on yet — municipal bonds.' Opening his file folder, he consulted a second sheet of notes. 'In the next six weeks, eleven issues of county and school district bonds within the state will be up for bid. If our bank fails to participate, at least half of those bonds are

certain to remain unsold.' Alex's voice sharpened: 'Is it the board's intention to dispense, so quickly after Ben Rosselli's death, with a tradition spanning three Rosselli generations?'

For the first time since the meeting began directors exchanged uneasy glances. A policy established long ago by the bank's founder, Giovanni Rosselli, had First Mercantile American Bank taking the lead in underwriting and selling bond issues of small municipalities in the state. Without such aid from (First Mercantile) the state's largest bank, such bond issues — never large, important, or well known — might go unmarketed, leaving financial needs of their communities unmet. The tradition had been faithfully adhered to by Giovanni's son, Lorenzo, and grandson Ben. The business was not especially profitable, though neither did it represent a loss. But it was a significant public service and also returned to small communities some of the money their own people deposited in First Mercantile.

'Jerome,' Leonard Kingswood suggested, 'maybe you should take another look at that situation.'

There were murmurs of assent.

Roscoe Heyward made a swift assessment. 'Jerome . . . if I may.'

The bank president nodded.

'In view of what seems a sentiment of the board,' Heyward offered smoothly, 'I'm certain we can make a fresh appraisal and perhaps restore a portion of municipal bond funding without impeding any of the Supranational arrangements. May I suggest that the board, having made its feelings clear, leaves details to the discretion of Jerome and myself.' Notably he did not include Alex.

Nods and voices signified agreement.

Alex objected, 'That's not a full commitment, nor does it do anything to restore home mortgages and small loans.'

The other board members were pointedly silent.

'I believe we've heard all viewpoints,' Jerome Patterton suggested. 'Perhaps we can now vote on the proposal as a whole.'

'No,' Alex said, 'there's still one other matter.' Patterton and Heyward exchanged glances of half-amused resignation.

'I've already pointed to a conflict of interest,' Alex stated somberly. 'Now I warn the board of an even larger one. Since negotiations of the Supranational loan, and up to yesterday afternoon, our own trust department has bought' — he consulted his notes — 'one hundred and twenty-three thousand Supranational shares. In that time, and almost certainly because of the substantial buying with our trust clients' money, the Supranational share price has risen seven and a half points, which I'm sure was intended and agreed to as a condition . . . '

He was drowned out by protesting voices — Roscoe Heyward's, Jerome Patterton's, and those of other directors.

Heyward was on his feet again, eyes blazing, 'That's a deliberate distortion!'

Alex slammed back, 'The purchasing is no distortion.'

'But your interpretation is. Supranational is an excellent investment for our trust accounts,' said Heyward.

'What makes it suddenly so good?' (Alex retorted).

Patterton protested heatedly, 'Alex, specific transactions of the trust department are not a matter for discussion here.'

Philip Johannsen snapped, 'I agree with that.'

Harold Austin and several others called out loudly, 'So do I'.

'Whether they are or aren't,' Alex persisted, 'I warn you all that what is happening may be in contravention of the Glass Steagall Act of 1933, and the directors can be held responsible . . . '

A half dozen more voices erupted angrily at once.

Above the other voices he continued firmly, 'I advise the board that if it ratifies the Supranational loan with all its ramifications, we'll regret it.' He leaned back in his chair. 'Thats all.'

Patterton, paler than before, announced, 'If there is no further discussion we will record a vote.'

Moments later the Supranational proposals were approved, with Alex the sole dissenter.

ANALYSIS OF THE DIALOGUE

Before reading further, undertake your own analysis of this series of tense interchanges. After giving a detailed analysis of the individual transactions, some conclusion will be drawn from the discussion.

Alex's first comment is Adult ego state behaviour, as it contains data which describes what he thinks, not how he feels. When he states 'to make the money available we're to cut mortgage lending' this involves problem analysis. The final sentence 'In these two areas alone the bank will be defective in its public service,' involves judgement behaviour, and also involves the Critical Parent.

The response of Patterton, 'It's been clearly stated that those cutbacks are temporary,' is on the surface rational and logical problem analysis. On a deeper level it is also an ulterior transaction from his Critical Parent, the implicit message being that Alex's analysis is incorrect. The data to support the evaluation comes from his non-verbal communication — the huffy way in which he replies.

To enable communication to continue, and avoid direct conflict, Alex uses a complementary transaction from his Adapted Child — 'Yes.' This enables him to return to his theme which is essentially Adult, involving further problem analysis. The comment 'In the next six weeks . . . ' is planning and organising, and anticipates the result of the bank's not participating in the municipal bond market. He also uses judgement behaviour, and concludes with problem analysis and implied control when he asks, 'Is it the board's intention to dispense, so quickly after Ben Rosselli's death, with a tradition spanning three Rosselli generations? The important message in this question however is ulterior Critical Parent, suggesting that tradition (interpersonal sensitivity is also shown by recognising this) should not be dispensed with and chastising the other board members for wanting to do so. The Critical Parent message is received and reacted to by the others present, who exchange uneasy glances; something which is typically Adapted Child behaviour. This is also an example of persuasiveness on the part of Alex.

Leonard Kingswood's comment, 'maybe you should take another look at that situation,' can be analysed on three of the Problem-Solving Dimensions. It shows interpersonal sensitivity to the board members' reaction and initiative on how to resolve the problem, as well as delegation of the problem to Jerome, the chairman, and as such is mainly Adult.

Roscoe Heyward's following comments also contain a considerable variety of behaviours. The statement 'Jerome . . . if I may' shows deference and sensitivity towards the chairman, and is Adapted Child behaviour. It paves the way for his Adult comments, 'In view of what seems a sentiment of the board . . . ' This is problem analysis and interpersonal sensitivity, and ends up with leadership when he says, 'May I suggest that the board, having made its feelings clear, leaves the details to the discretion of Jerome and myself.' This passage also shows flexibility in responding to the problem originally raised by Alex.

Alex's interjection is Critical Parent, and shows judgement when he says 'That's not a full commitment, nor does it do anything to restore home mortgages and small loans.'

The response of the chairman, 'I believe we've heard all viewpoints. Perhaps we can now vote on the proposal as a whole,' contains judgement and leadership. From the point of view of the ego states it is Critical Parent, even if delivered in a rational and seemingly Adult manner.

This is then crossed by Alex's transaction, which is Critical Parent — 'No' — and also later when he says, 'Now I warn the board', after which he provided data from the Adult ego state, 'Our own trust department has bought one hundred and twenty-three thousand Supranational shares.' His ensuing comments about the rise in share price contain problem analysis and judgement. The detailed figures given by him of one hundred and twenty-three thousand shares and a share price rise of seven and a half points indicate attention to detail. This is also an example of tenacity.

The protesting voices, and especially Roscoe Heyward's comment, 'That's a deliberate distortion,' seems like an angry Child outburst. The response of Alex, 'The purchasing is no distortion,' is on the surface his

Adult ego state providing judgement, but can be interpreted as ulterior Critical Parent, implying that the facts speak for themselves, and that Roscoe is wrong in suggesting it is a distortion. The two men continue with a series of further crossed transactions, until Jerome Patterton interrupts them with a Critical Parent comment, 'Alex, specific transactions of the trust department are not a matter for discussion here.' This is an example of management control. Despite the continued opposition to his view, Alex sticks to his point with, 'I warn you all that what is happening may be a contravention of the Glass Steagall Act . . . I advise the board that if it ratifies the Supranational loan with all its ramifications we'll regret it.' This is a mixture of Critical Parent, telling the board not to go ahead with the loan, and Adult, when he uses further problem analysis to spell out the legal implications of going ahead. Again, it shows tenacity in sticking to his views.

DRAWING CONCLUSIONS ABOUT INDIVIDUAL BEHAVIOUR PATTERNS

The detailed analysis can be considered on a number of levels. For purposes of demonstrating the value of Behaviour Technology, it will be used to draw conclusions about individual behaviour in three different areas: the individuals' Problem-Solving Dimension profile, the overall ego state and transaction profiles, and then on a deeper level the games that are being played here.

If we quantify the Problem-Solving Dimensions used by the main participants in the board meeting we end up with the following conclusions:

Alex: High use of – problem analysis, judgement, tenacity.
           Some use of – planning and organising, attention to detail, control, persuasiveness, interpersonal sensitivity.
Jerome: Some use of – judgement, problem analysis, leadership, control.
Roscoe: High use of – judgement
           Some use of – problem analysis, leadership, interpersonal sensitivity, flexibility.
Leonard: Some use of – interpersonal sensitivity, delegation, initiative, problem analysis.

Alex's behaviour is mostly task orientated, and contains higher problem analysis and judgement than any of the others in the meeting. Apart from the one incident when he refers to the tradition of the bank to take up municipal bonds, his behaviour is largely concerned with data and its implications. Other board members in contrast show less concern with the

facts about the loan than Alex, but show interpersonal sensitivity and
leadership in the group. Significantly the designated chairman, Jerome,
shows less leadership and delegation than his colleague Roscoe.

While the Problem-Solving Dimensions show us the distribution of
problem-solving behaviours within the group, they do not do justice to the
expression of feelings. For this side of the picture we need to refer to the
ego states and transaction analysis. The ego states in evidence in this
discussion are:

Alex: High Critical Parent, high Adult, low Adapted Child.
Jerome: Some Critical Parent, some Adult.
Roscoe: Some Critical Parent, some Free and Adapted Child.
Leonard: Some Adult.

This perspective of the conversation shows how much Critical Parent
discussion took place, and why there was such a large amount of controversy. This is reinforced by the fact that all board members who spoke
engaged in some form of crossed transaction with Alex.

On a different level this discussion can be considered from the point of
view of the games which were played. Two games appear to be going on
here, Cornered and Uproar. By pushing his view, which was obviously not
in agreement with other board members, Alex is setting himself up to be
put down by the other board members. After the chairman says, 'I believe
we've heard all viewpoints. Perhaps we can now vote . . . ', Alex intervenes
again with 'No, there's still one other matter,' which then leads to a series
of crossed transactions. The evidence from the text is that the final effect
of this is to create further distance between Alex and the others present,
rather than to get them to change their views. The animated responses of
the other board members suggest that they want to get Alex 'cornered'.
When Alex is ruled out of court for raising the purchase of Supranational
shares by Jerome Patterton — 'Alex, specific transactions of the trust
department are not a matter for discussion here' — the way that this
comment is supported by the others who voiced their support for this
suggestion indicates that the board were attempting to 'corner' Alex; and
recognition by Alex that this has been successfully achieved comes in his
final resigned comment, after leaning back in his chair — 'Thats all.'
Evidence also suggests that the board were playing Uproar rather than
looking at the facts of the case.

With these three perspectives we can now evaluate the effectiveness of
the meeting. The evidence suggests that in many ways it could have been
improved. The overall outcome is that a decision was made to go ahead
with the loan, while isolating one of the board members. Relatively little
problem-solving took place during the meeting, which to a large extent was
governed by feelings and sentiment, rather than by data. It is also notice-

able how little part the chairman played in leading and controlling the discussion, or in attempting to resolve the differences around the table.

OPTIONS FOR BEHAVIOUR CHANGE

It would be interesting to speculate on the effect if different behaviours had been adopted by the three main participants in the board meeting, Alex, Jerome and Roscoe. Each of these participants might well have altered the form and outcome of the meeting, if they had adopted other behaviour options that were available to them.

The impact of the chairman, Jerome, on the meeting was low. His only real contribution was to bring discussion to a close so that a vote could be taken on the Supranational loan. One option open to him would have been to encourage more Adult discussion of the objections raised by Alex, rather than to cut him short and bring the matter to the vote. After Alex said, 'That's not a full commitment, nor does it do anything to restore home mortgages and small loans,' Jerome had the option of continuing to use Adult behaviour and more problem analysis to get to the bottom of the issues raised. Something like, 'Before we deal with that issue in detail, Alex, are there any other concerns you have in connection with the loan?' might have steered the discussion on to a more analytical and logical course, and avoided the crossed transactions that occurred later.

Another option open to Jerome would have been to use more Critical Parent in handling Alex. By using the phrase, 'I believe we've heard all viewpoints,' he was allowing Alex an opportunity to get back into the conversation. Instead he might have said, 'We've discussed this long enough and I want to bring this to the vote. Will all those in favour of the loan raise their hands.' Such a statement would have contained more Critical Parent and management control and would have ended the discussion there and then. To have raised an objection Alex would have to challenge openly the authority of the chairman to lead the meeting.

The outcome of the meeting might also have been changed by Alex himself. Much of his behaviour consisted of high levels of judgement coupled with problem analysis. Because the judgements were largely opposed by the other board members it is not surprising that they challenged the basis of these with their own judgements. The one occasion when Alex successfully changed the course of the meeting was when he showed interpersonal sensitivity to the traditions of the bank of taking up municipal bonds. By using the same strategy a few moments later in the discussion he might have been able to change board members' views on other issues as well. He could for example have acknowledged his success by thanking the members of the board for taking this into account, and then used this as a platform to introduce his concern about the purchase of the Supranational shares. In the place of his Critical Parent objection, 'That's not a full commitment, nor does it do anything to restore home mortgages and small loans,' he might have said, 'I am pleased that Jerome and Roscoe will restore a portion of the municipal bond funding, and I'm sure the board's decision will be valued by many of our customers. Nevertheless there is another concern I would like to bring to the board's attention, and that is . . . '. This Adapted Child acknowledgement might well have created a more positive atmosphere, and enabled him to continue with parallel adult transactions, rather than crossed transactions in which, as was evident, real communication ceased.

When raising the contravention of the Glass Steagall Act, Alex might have done so in another way. By touching first on the sensitive issue of the purchase of Supranational shares and their resultant rise in price he antagonised his audience, even though he was using problem analysis. By showing more interpersonal sensitivity before undertaking his problem analysis he might have convinced the others that he had a valid case. For example he might have said, 'I would like to make you aware of the requirements of the Glass Steagall Act, and the implications this has for our dealing in Supranational shares . . . ' Only after he had stated the requirements of the Act and its implications for the directors would he have gone on to consider the share purchase issue. Such behavioural tactics might have brought about more parallel transactions and problem analysis in the place of the large number of crossed transactions and purely judgement behaviour.

It was interesting to contrast the behaviour shown towards the chairman, and towards Alex, by Roscoe. Towards the chairman he demonstrated considerable interpersonal sensitivity from both his Adult and Adapted Child. Towards Alex, however, no interpersonal sensitivity was shown, and in its place he used a lot of judgement, all of it coming from his Critical Parent. If in its place he had used the Nurturing Parent to encourage Alex to make his case, or problem analysis so that the issues could be fully debated, the meeting might have been more harmonious, as well as coming to a decision based on more data.

The alternative behaviour options available to the characters in Arthur Hailey's book are not put forward with the intention of improving the plot. They are intended to demonstrate the variety of behaviours that are open to us to choose from in any given real life situation. In the same way that these lead characters could have behaved differently, so also might we, in the variety of interactions and transactions we had last week. While you may well have been satisfied with many of these transactions, there may be others from which you might have desired a different outcome. The objective of Behaviour Technology is to assist the analysis of those situations, and then help us to identify and adopt the most appropriate options for solving the behaviour problems we encounter.

REFERENCE

1) Hailey, A., *The Money Changers*, Michael Joseph Ltd, in association
    with Souvenir Press Ltd, 1975.

PART TWO

BEHAVIOUR TECHNOLOGY IN ACTION

4 Defining performance requirements

This chapter deals with what is probably the most underrated cause of human resource problems in organisations; inadequate definition of performance requirements. After reviewing the traditional approach to defining job performance requirements, an approach based on Behaviour Technology will be proposed. This has considerable practical potential in helping to prevent and solve many work problems.

Before embarking on this path, let us consider the possible benefits of defining job performance requirements. In most organisations, the definition of job performance requirements occurs in the form of a job description. In some large companies, whole teams and departments are dedicated to analysing the jobs of others in the organisation, so that a complete library of these descriptions is always available. The apparent purpose of writing job descriptions is often the satisfaction of some personnel regulation which makes them a requirement before authorisation to recruit or promote is given. Once the job description has been produced in the appropriate style, the recruiting manager can proceed to attract and evaluate candidates without giving further consideration to the job description. The description of a job given orally to interview candidates sometimes bears little resemblance to the job description produced to justify the recruitment exercise.

Although job descriptions are conventionally regarded as the most common method of defining job performance requirements, they are by no means the only method, or even the best method of doing this. Alternative methods are available such as that prepared by Rosemary Stewart,[1] described later on, or techniques such as the Position Analysis Questionnaire. It is the author's view that the concept of a 'job description' is itself a misunderstanding of what jobs are concerned with in organisations. The essence of any job is how it contributes to the enterprise; if it does not contribute, then the job is misconceived. For this reason, the term 'job performance requirements' is intentionally used, as it focuses attention on the performance or contribution the job provides to the business.

The key question is how defined job performance requirements can help businesses achieve their objectives. Are they of value for tackling human resource problems or do they merely fill up space in filing cabinets in the personnel department? Before reading further, reflect on the real use made of job descriptions in the organisations you have known.

THE BENEFITS OF DEFINING JOB PERFORMANCE REQUIREMENTS

A precise definition of job performance requirements can provide many tangible benefits. If we understand the performance requirements of a job, we are more likely to be successful in selecting someone who can perform the job effectively. Knowing that a job involves detailed design of micro-electronic circuits has implications for the type of person we are likely to want to attract and then select for a job. A clear picture of the performance requirements of a job will give us an idea of the attributes required of candidates. In some jobs, these may seem obvious from the title alone, for example we might assume that a financial accountant needs to have a qualification in accountancy and some experience in working in this field. However, the problem then arises of deciding on the level of formal qualifications in accountancy that is required, as well as the amount of experience. The job may also have requirements that have no bearing on technical accounting skills, e.g. supervision of subordinates, or influencing skills with line management. We can therefore conclude that a job title alone will give little indication of the type of job holder requirement. A more detailed description of the performance requirements is therefore necessary. Defining performance requirements can also help in other parts of the recruitment process, including the writing of job advertisements, as a vehicle for describing the job to likely candidates, and as a pointer to where likely candidates are to be found.

The basis of many salary reward systems also depends on an evaluation of the relative performance requirements of jobs in the organisation. This process, usually referred to as job evaluation, consists of an assessment of the relative worth of a job to all others in the company. Remuneration and benefits can then be allocated to job holders according to their value to the organisation. The principle usually used is that holders of jobs which are deemed to contribute more to the organisation (and which tend to have more demanding job performance requirements) are given greater rewards. As well as facilitating internal company comparisons, an assessment of performance requirements can make comparison possible with the rewards offered for similar jobs in other organisations, and in different countries. A clear picture of the performance requirements of jobs in an organisation can serve as a basis for managing salary and benefits systems.

Defining job performance requirements may also have positive spin-offs for the performance of the job holder. If we have a clear idea of what others expect of us (and in particular our boss!) we are more likely to be able to fulfil those expectations.

Defined performance requirements can also be useful in relation to training to improve job performance. Employees are often sent on training courses in the hope that they will become more effective. While this is a laudable intention, the effort which goes into assessing that the individual does have a performance deficiency in the skills being developed by the training course, or even that these skills really are required for effective performance, is often very low. Large numbers of employees are sent on leadership and presentation skills training programmes of all types. All too often attendance occurs on the assumption that improved leadership and presentation skills are important. While the development of these skills may be constructive, the practical benefit to be gained from their development is frequently vaguely understood and ill-defined. The clear definition of performance requirements can provide criteria against which employee job performance can be assessed, and then training and development needs defined. If a manager consistently fails to achieve time deadlines this may be attributable to his or her lack of planning and organising but it may instead be due to their poor problem analysis, a lack of delegation, or poor management control skills. We need to acknowledge that poor achievement of objectives can be due to a variety of possible behaviour deficiencies. We are only likely to identify the real reasons for job performance deficiency if we consider employee behaviours against those that are required for effective performance. The benefit of defined performance requirements is that they provide a clear and precise yardstick against which individual managers' performance can be assessed, and skill gaps can be evaluated. More will be said about this in Chapter 10.

A further benefit of defining job performance requirements is in the area of organisation development. Evaluation of the performance skills in a particular department or unit can be helpful when developing groups within the organisation. As with individual training, defined performance requirements provide broad criteria for developing the careers of groups of managers. This is also considered in the chapter on developing manpower (Chapter 10).

While the potential benefits of defining job performance requirements may seem great, you may well have doubts about them. This is understandable when we review the conventional approach that has been taken towards this issue. Job performance requirements are set out in a job description which takes the form of a list of key tasks or duties. While this may give an overall picture of what is involved in a job, it gives very little idea of the precise job behaviour required of the job holder.

Typical statements of tasks or duties may take the form of: 'undertake day to day supervision of the clerical department' or 'provide market survey reports of the pharmaceutical industry'. Such statements fail to provide a precise idea of the outputs of the job, and they give no indication of the behaviours required for effective performance. As a result, it is difficult if not impossible to use these types of job description for many of the purposes described above. In order to yield selection criteria against which candidates can be assessed, a job description needs to describe the precise behaviours required for effective job performance. If the job performance of a manager is to be assessed, the assessment must be made against precise criteria — the outputs or end results of the manager's activities and the behaviours he needs to use to achieve them. If the statement of outputs is omitted it becomes impossible to ascertain whether overall objectives have been achieved or not, and if the statement of behaviours is omitted it becomes impossible to assess what it is the manager did or did not do which determined his or her success, or lack of it. Statements of duties or general activities fall vaguely between behaviours and outputs, and thus are inefficient methods of describing job performance requirements.

If the duty of a marketing manager is to provide market surveys, this could be interpreted in a variety of ways. It could refer to the summarising of information already available from other sources in the company. At the other extreme, it could involve commissioning market research surveys for discovering long-term business needs. As well as involving different amounts of discretion for resources, these alternative interpretations of the same task are likely to require completely different types of behaviours by the job holder. The summarising of information already available inside the company would primarily require a moderate level of problem analysis for comprehending and summarising data and an ability to present the summary either verbally or in writing, i.e. persuasiveness. The commissioning of market research surveys, however, may well require negotiating with market research agencies, planning and organising how the project will be tackled, judgement of the proposals put forward by different agencies, and the allocation and control of resources required for the survey, as well as problem analysis at a higher level than would be required for just summarising information already available in the company. We can thus appreciate how a duties statement often fails to provide a meaningful description of the performance requirements of a job.

MORE ADVANCED METHODS OF DEFINING JOB PERFORMANCE REQUIREMENTS

More recently, organisations on both sides of the Atlantic have started to use more sophisticated forms of job description than those which merely contain lists of key tasks and reporting relationships. The approach developed by Hay Management Consultants[1], for example, describes jobs under the headings of 'purpose', 'dimensions', 'nature and scope' and 'principal accountabilities', of which the last two contain much detailed information. The 'nature and scope' considers what is involved in meeting the outputs of the job, and includes factors such as location in the organisation, supporting staff, job knowledge, the nature of problem-solving, and freedom to make decisions. The principal accountabilities refer to the end results that are required from a job. This approach is more comprehensive than the traditional one, and provides a more detailed picture of what is involved in a job.

As the Hay approach gives a clear indication of the outputs required from a job, this overcomes one of the major shortcomings of traditional job descriptions. Nevertheless, this approach does not provide a precise indication of the job behaviours required for successful performance. Some indication of these may be given in the nature and scope section, but this is insufficient to provide a full specification of what the job holder must actually do to achieve the principle outputs of the job.

Although the job descriptions of organisations now indicate performance requirements from the point of view of outputs, most fail to define performance requirements from the point of view of the specific behaviours required to achieve them. It should come as little surprise therefore that the job descriptions produced in many organisations seldom receive much attention once they have been produced. Managers with line responsibilities often regard job descriptions as of marginal value to the business. The production of job descriptions is seen as tedious, time-consuming and of little consequence, apart from keeping the bureaucrats in personnel happy. Once produced and authorised, the job description languishes in a personnel file, solely as a momento to the intentions of those responsible for formulating personnel regulations.

Defining the behaviour requirements of a job depends on a clear understanding of the outputs of a job and the work situations from which the outputs are produced. Rosemary Stewart[2] concluded from her investigation that jobs can be analysed in four dimensions:

1. Contact type (the nature of job relationships);
2. Work pattern (task structure);
3. Exposure (risk of visibility of poor performance);
4. Choices (the options and alternatives open to the job holder).

Let us consider the earlier example of a marketing manager who is required to provide market surveys which he initiates and commissions from external market research agencies. Using Rosemary Stewart's dimensions, the job could be assessed to involve relationships in and outside the organisations; work of a project nature; a degree of exposure depending on the decisions that are made as a result of the market surveys; as well as a variety of choices in terms of the alternative types of market research survey that could be commissioned, and the agency that is chosen to undertake the work. If the marketing manager's company had a policy of using only one market research agency, this would limit his choices, as well as the diversity of his relationships outside the company. If the company also had laid down policies on the types of market research it commissioned, i.e. quantitative as opposed to qualitative, this would further reduce the choices open to the job holder, as well as having implications for the work pattern required.

THE BEHAVIOUR TECHNOLOGY APPROACH TO JOB PERFORMANCE REQUIREMENTS

The Behaviour Technology definition of job performance requirements involves two main components:

1. A specification of the task outputs that the job holder is expected to achieve, which contribute to the business;
2. A description of the behaviours that the job holder will need to use in order to achieve the specified task outputs.

In practice there is rarely only one set of behaviours that will enable a job holder to achieve a given set of task outputs. Nevertheless any given task usually involves certain minimum behaviours, which if not used make it impossible to achieve the task output. The relationship between task outputs and the behaviours needed to fulfil them is best illustrated by returning to the previous example of a marketing manager.

If the company left decisions on market research entirely to the discretion of the marketing manager, this would place more behaviour demands on the job holder than if he or she had to operate within existing policies in terms of which agency to use, the type of market research projects which the company commissioned, etc. A marketing manager who operated without any policy constraints on market research would need to engage in more problem analysis, judgement, and planning when commissioning research than one who was forced to use a specified agency and only one research method. The ego states required by the manager who operated without predetermined policies or guidelines would be different from those required by one who had to operate within them. In the former case, the manager would require more Little Professor behaviours with which to cope with the variety of options and choices open to him. In contrast, a marketing manager who operated within rigidly defined policies for market research would need to use more Adapted Child behaviours, so that he or she could conform to these policies.

Thus someone who might be highly effective in a marketing job without policies and procedures might be constrained and as a result dissatisfied with a job which had strictly laid down procedures. Alternatively, an individual who would be competent and satisfied with the latter job might be ineffective and feel out of his or her depth in the unstructured job. This analysis shows the very great diversity that can occur between jobs with the same title and even the same overall duties. It demonstrates the very real value of defining the behaviour requirements of a job in order to understand it. The benefits of defining job performance requirements for selection, job development and training, as well as overall management development, all depend on the identification of behaviour patterns necessary to achieve the outputs of the job. If these are omitted, the real practical value of the job description is limited merely to job evaluation and objective setting. Not surprisingly, once these benefits have been achieved the job description is forgotten, as it is unable to serve further practical purpose.

Table 4.1

JOB PERFORMANCE REQUIREMENTS DEFINITION

Position: Personnel Manager

Organisation Context
Reports to: General Manager
Functional reporting to: Company Personnel Director
Direct reports: 2 Personnel Officers
                       1 Secretary/Administrator
Provides service to: 700 employees, of which 400 are junior staff,
                       300 senior
Salary bill: £9M
Union agreement: ASTMS for all staff
Business of unit: Manufacturing, technical development, sales and
                       marketing
Turnover: £25M

Output/Performance Requirements

1. Work with other senior managers in formulating business plans for the overall management and direction of the unit.
2. Provide a manpower plan for the business, taking account of line business objectives, which specifies number and quality of human resources required in the long and short term, so that personnel priorities can be identified.
3. Formulate and implement personnel practices and procedures which take account of business plans and company personnel policies, and aim for the optimum deployment of human resources in the company.
4. Administer reward systems for all jobs in the unit in accordance with company compensation guidelines, systematically and equitably so as to attract, retain and motivate employees to perform their jobs effectively within human resource budget constraints.

5. Attract and select new employees from the specification of require-
    ments to induction, to ensure that departments have the necessary
    manpower required to achieve business objectives.
6. Advise line managers on the structure and resourcing of their depart-
    ments so that the most effective deployment of human resources can
    occur, in line with business needs.
7. Assist managers on issues of safety, grievance, discipline and other
    personnel issues, so that company policies, legal requirements and
    community standards are adhered to.
8. Assist line managers resolve employee relations problems both of a
    formal and informal type, so that a positive and harmonious
    employee climate prevails.
9. Guide and structure development and promotion activities in the
    unit so that the aspirations of employees and company manpower
    requirements can best be met.
10. Monitor the deployment of human resources, from termination,
    recruitment and salary costs, absenteeism, etc., to identify where
    remedial line or personnel action is required to optimise the use of
    human resources in the achievement of business objectives.

Behaviour Requirements: problem-solving dimensions

1. Problem analysis — required for creating manpower plans, resourcing,
    administration, and employee relations, including use of professional
    techniques.
2. Judgement — required on people and human resource problems,
    implications of manpower plan, advising on structure, resourcing,
    development, grievances, etc. This will need to take account of com-
    pany practices and professional and legal requirements.
3. Management control — will require setting up standards for personnel
    operations and adherence to these, e.g. procedures for salary changes,
    promotion criteria, union agreements and monitoring human resources.
4. Interpersonal sensitivity — required overall to people in the business,
    and to the role of personnel as an advisory function.
5. Planning and organising — for setting own/subordinate priorities, and
    getting managers to play their part in these.
6. Attention to detail — required for administration, manpower plans,
    personnel records, where high levels of information are required.
7. Initiative — leading in human resource problem solving.

TA ego states

Nurturing Parent: Moderate amount required for counselling employees
                   at all levels. Must not be too large, otherwise would
                   take employees' side too easily.

Critical Parent: Moderate amount required to ensure adherence to rules, especially when managers attempt to bypass rules. Too small CP would not allow this to occur, too large would be counter productive for staff role.

Adult: Large amount needed for divergent role, from solving complex long-term human resource problems to counselling individuals.

Adapted Child: Moderate to large required. Necessary for working within company guidelines and accepting advisory role vis-à-vis line management.

Free Child: Moderate required for use in relation to managers at all levels.

The job performance requirements for a personnel manager are given in Table 4.1. This has been condensed to demonstrate how performance requirements can be summarised without the need for a lengthy dissertation. Managers are often not interested in long screeds, and if a definition of job performance requirements is to be read, brevity is of the essence. The Job Performance Requirements Definition is divided into three sections:

1.   The organisation context;
2.   The output or performance requirements;
3.   The behaviour requirements.

The organisation context contains verifiable factual data about the reporting relationships, costs and quantitative data. It sets the scene within which the job exists.

The output requirements statements each describe major areas where the job needs to achieve results or outcomes. Where practicable, they contain the most important action verb through which the job holder will achieve these outcomes, e.g. create, advise, administer, assist etc. The performance requirements statements also describe constraints, factors and issues which the job holder will need to take account of, e.g. 'in accordance with company compensation policies', 'from the specification of requirements to induction', or 'taking account of business objectives'. The final part of each performance requirements statement should contain some justification of why the requirement exists at all. Examples which occur in the personnel manager performance requirements statements include: 'so that personnel priorities can be identified,' and 'so that a positive and harmonious employee relations climate prevails'.

The unique part of the Job Performance Requirements Definition is the statement of behaviour requirements. This describes the required behaviours in terms of the Problem-Solving Dimensions and TA ego states which the job holder will need to use if he or she is to fulfil the performance requirements. While it is relatively easy to *describe* these with TA and the PSDs, it is a much more difficult matter to identify with precision those behaviours that are most required for successful achievement of the job outputs. Unless this statement of behaviour requirements reflects reality, the exercise becomes pointless.

Having argued the case for including behaviour requirements as part of the Job Performance Requirements Definition, we now need to consider how this can be achieved in a practical and meaningful way.

The framework described in Chapter 2, based on Transactional Analysis and the Problem-Solving Dimensions, can be shown to be effective for describing the behaviours required to perform a job. The key difficulty is to identify initially those behaviours which are consistently required for achieving the outputs of the job, as opposed to those which may only characterise a particular job holder even though they do not contribute significantly to effective performance. We also need to eliminate from our analysis those behaviours which are required infrequently and so can be disregarded. The task is a complex one, as much of what we do often has little consequence while only a small proportion of our actions is critical in influencing what we achieve.

IDENTIFYING JOB REQUIREMENTS BY OBSERVATION

The most obvious method of identifying the behaviours that are required for effective job performance is direct observation. A trained observer can travel with a job holder and record details of his behaviour, and later analyse this in terms of TA and the PSDs. The value of this approach is that the job analyst can observe behaviours which the job holder themselves might be completely unaware of. Many of us take parts of our job for granted and may forget to raise these if asked to describe our job. This applies particularly to routine behaviour which we take for granted.

Despite the potential accuracy of this approach, it is very costly and might involve the analyst in observing a job holder over a considerable period to ensure that the behaviours noted are typical; also the fact of observation can itself alter the behaviour of the job holder. Most of us behave differently if we know we are being watched; we may be much more unlikely to spend time joking with colleagues, or to reprimand subordinates harshly if we know someone is assiduously observing our every move!

Direct observation on its own is most likely to be appropriate for jobs that have short cycle times, e.g. on a manufacturing plant or in a clerical department, where observations over few hours will provide sufficient representative samples of the behaviours required in that job. Because senior management jobs frequently involve drawn out activities, obtaining a representative sample of job behaviours may take many weeks of observation. Despite the cost of undertaking this type of observation, if an entire company's senior management development programme depended on understanding the required behaviours of senior managers, the expense may be more than justified.

When an observer tracks the behaviour of a job holder, this involves two basic procedures. The first stage involves merely writing down what the employee says or does as it happens. Only after the observation is over will the record of events be categorised into the Problem-Solving Dimensions and TA ego states. The separation of recording from categorising and evaluation leads to a much more effective evaluation being made because it enables us to concentrate on one activity at a time. Often when we evaluate what others say as they are talking, the result is that we fail to take in everything that is being said because we are concentrating on evaluating what was said a moment before. We are, therefore, much more likely to obtain a detailed analysis of what someone says or does if we separate the evaluation from the recording process. This problem is considered in more detail in the chapter on assessment centres (Chapter 9).

Once a complete set of behaviour data is collected, the analyst will need to identify those behaviours which contributed to the successful achievement of objectives, and separate these from the behaviours which did not, so that the final report can indicate required as opposed to optional or undesirable behaviours.

IDENTIFYING JOB REQUIREMENTS BY INTERVIEW

The more common method of analysing jobs is by interviewing the job holder. Enquiring about the things that take up most of a manager's time, that present greatest difficulty, the types of meetings attended, the most important objectives, etc., all yield insight into what a job holder does. To obtain valid behavioural data, the job analyst needs to ask probing questions such as: 'Tell me what you did,' or 'What part did you play in . . .'. By concentrating on the critical incidents or situations facing the job holder, the interviewer can elicit what he or she actually did.

Conventionally, job analysts pay most attention to the duties and outcomes of a job. The Behaviour Technology approach also involves obtaining data on what a person actually does in terms of task behaviours as well as through expressing feelings. Obtaining such data and analysing it is however a complex and demanding task and as in direct observations, the processes of obtaining and recording behavioural data need to be separated from the analysis and classification processes. During the interview itself, the job analyst should concentrate exclusively on the first two and only afterwards should he classify his observations into the Problem-Solving Dimensions and TA ego states.

Data on the behaviours required for successful job performance can also be obtained from interviews with the job holder's superiors, by asking such questions as 'Think of an incident when your subordinate performed very well,' followed by 'What did she/he do that resulted in effective perform-ance?' or 'Think of an incident when your subordinate was ineffective — what did she/he do or not do that caused this?'. Specific behaviours can be related to the essential outputs of a job by questions such as 'What are the most important things you want this person to achieve?' and 'What does the job holder have to do to achieve the standard of work required?'.

Interviews with job holders, their bosses, subordinates or colleagues are likely to be far less time consuming than actual observation of the job holder. Nevertheless they do take time. If the definition of job behaviour requirements applies to a large number of jobs it may well be appropriate to obtain some data on the behaviours exhibited by different job holders.

Rather than conducting interviews, it may be appropriate to use a questionnaire instead. A questionnaire could involve ranking the Problem-Solving Dimensions, or completion of a forced choice TA questionnaire. Such questionnaires can be easily administered and provide data from job holders and those who work with them. A particular advantage of this method is that it increases the sample of people from whom data is obtained and thus helps to gain the commitment of those involved as regards the end results of the job analysis exercise. This is especially important where it is intended that management use the definition of job performance behaviours as a basis for decision-making. Unless managers agree with the results of a job analysis exercise, there is little likelihood, however accurate it may be, that it will serve any positive purpose for the business. This problem confronts the use of many professional techniques and methods. However relevant and helpful a technique may be, if those involved in using it have no faith in it it can bring about no real benefits. It may therefore be useful to obtain additional data from other job holders, as well as gaining the commitment of interested parties to use a behavioural questionnaire to support data already obtained from direct observation and interviews. Inevitably, questionnaires are even further removed from behaviour itself than a job analysis interview, but they do have advantages of economy of administration.

Having proposed comprehensive methods of defining job performance requirements based on job outputs and on the employee behaviours necessary to achieve these, we now need to review the extent to which this technique is relevant and applicable. To produce defined performance requirements by this means will be more time and resource consuming than conventional methods. The justification of this approach depends entirely on the organisational benefits achieved. When a company purchases a piece of capital equipment or indeed when we buy a new automobile, it is normal for a technical specification of the machine's performance to be provided; the Behaviour Technology method of defining job performance requirements is similar to a mechanical specification setting out a level of performance. Instead of giving brake horse power, compression ratios or power to weight ratios, all of which result in a certain top speed, acceleration and miles per gallon performance, job performance requirements as defined by Behaviour Technology describe how certain job outputs can be achieved from specified behaviours. In some cases we may not need to have a full description of the mechanical specification, and equally for some jobs there may be no benefit to be derived from defining required job behaviours. Nevertheless, the number of problems faced by organisations today suggest that the benefits from defining job performance requirements may make the exercise more than worthwhile.

A major impact of equal opportunity legislation in the United States and, to a lesser extent, in Britain and other countries, has been to force employers to justify selection and recruitment decisions. The thread running through most of this legislation is that employers need to be able to show that a candidate who is not selected for a job cannot fulfil the behaviours required for that job as well as the selected candidate. The number of successful cases brought by individuals against large corporations for unfair discrimination demonstrate that the behavioural requirements for achieving job outputs have often not been adequately defined. Selection decisions based on psychological tests are particularly coming under attack as it is so difficult to demonstrate beyond reasonable doubt that job performance is related to scores achieved on a pencil and paper test.

The Behaviour Technology approach to job requirements definition provides precise demonstrable criteria against which candidates can be assessed. Often employers state educational qualification requirements for employees. While educational achievement is generally related to intelligence levels it may not be so for underprivileged groups, and in these cases would not be a reliable predictor of job performance. By stating that certain specified levels of problem analysis, judgement, or planning and organising are required, it becomes a much more empirical process to evaluate whether a candidate can or cannot achieve the required standard. It is for this reason that selection and promotion decisions based on Behaviour Technology are much less likely to be open to charges of unfair discrimination.

Another problem encountered frequently in large companies is the question of improving employee performance. Despite the use of a variety of techniques, ranging from management by objectives to all manner of performance appraisal and review systems, it is very difficult to assist employees to develop their job performance. One of the greates obstacles in this is that while expected job outputs are increasingly becoming defined, most of us find it very difficult to know precisely what we need to do to achieve these outputs. The proper definition of job performance requirements in terms of behaviour, however, provides a basis for such a discussion. More will be said about this approach in the chapter dealing with performance improvement (Chapter 6).

While the approach to defining job performance requirements proposed in this chapter is rigorous and resource consuming, it has significant advantages over the alternative methods available. By defining the actual behaviour of an employee in terms of the Problem-Solving Dimensions and TA ego states, it becomes practicable to identify whether a particular person can perform a given job or what he or she needs to do differently to perform it more effectively.

REFERENCES

1)   Rawlinson, J., 'Writing Job Descriptions,' *Marketing*, Feb., 1980.
2)   Stewart, R., *Contrasts in Management*, McGraw-Hill, 1976.

5   Assessment interviewing

Almost everyone who has a job will have been interviewed as part of the selection process. Despite its widespread use as a method of assessment, the available evidence suggests that the interview is a highly unreliable device. This chapter reviews the use of the job interview and the changes that have taken place in interviewing strategy. An interviewing method based on Behaviour Technology will then be proposed which can significantly enhance our use of this established technique so that it can provide more and better data with which to make selection decisions.

The selection interview can serve a number of purposes. As well as being an assessment device as to whether a candidate can perform a job, the interview can also provide an opportunity for the employer to sell both the job and the organisation to the potential employee, or to negotiate terms and conditions of employment. Judging from the way some interviewers behave, the interview can, in some instances, serve as an opportunity for the interviewer to inflate his own feelings of importance and worth (from either a Critical Parent or Child point of view). This seems to be apparent when the interviewer does more talking than the candidate: a situation you may well have experienced on some occasion! Despite these and other possible functions, the concern of this chapter is on the assessment aspects of the interview, dealing with the gathering of data as a basis for making a judgement about whether a candidate is suitable for dealing with a job or career path.

As the most widely used method of employee assessment, the job interview can have a key impact on business results, as selection decisions are one of the most important types of human resource decisions made by organisations. By taking on employees who perform their jobs effectively and have potential for fulfilling other jobs in the future, an organisation is making a vital contribution to its own survival and growth. In today's environment, human resource costs form the largest single element of many organisations' costs, so the selection of employees is a major investment decision.

It is against this background that the assessment interview should be considered. The importance of conducting the interview in a way which enables correct recruitment decisions to be made is much greater than is usually appreciated. The objective of gathering data about the candidate so that an accurate prediction can be made about his or her job performance is simple to state, but difficult to achieve. The remainder of the chapter will review how this is usually done and how it can be done more effectively.

THE CONVENTIONAL WISDOM OF SELECTION INTERVIEWING

Interview assessment has traditionally been concerned with one specific job or type of job. However, organisations now increasingly recruit individuals for their potential to take on other jobs in the future. This applies particularly to recruitment of young entrants from university or school where selection is intended not merely to fill up places on the organisation's intake programme, but rather to provide manpower to fill junior and middle management and technical positions five or more years in the future.

The majority of interview assessments up to some twenty years ago were almost entirely based on the impact made by the candidate on the interviewer. Comments such as: 'Her face will fit,' 'We can't take him because he wears suede shoes,' 'people with moustaches are dishonest,' are based on the impact the candidate made on the interviewer, and are almost entirely subjective.

Impact evaluations about others can be based on a variety of causes. The typical assessment of 'his/her face fits' may be based on the fact that the impact of an individual concurs with that typical of other employees in the company. Some organisations seem to have a predominance of independent, tough and rugged types (Free Child and Critical Parent). Other organisations have a predominance of critical intellectual problem-solvers who possess high problem-solving and management control skills. Other organisations are staffed by conformist achievers (Adapted Child and Adult). Selection of an individual whose 'face fits' will tend to perpetuate the company culture and value system but may not assist the fulfilment of company objectives. For example, to recruit highly intelligent individuals to fulfil all the junior jobs in an organisation is a recipe for disaster, as is the perpetual recruitment of conformists into a research department. Selection needs to take account of the specific behaviours required for performance of the vacant job, rather than some generalised company norm.

Despite the fact that impact assessments are largely subjective, they may have some value. In jobs which involve considerable contact with others, e.g. salesman, personnel officer, airline steward/ess, the initial impact made by an individual on others may be critical for their effective performance of the job. Therefore it may be a valid requirement that the candidate should make a favourable initial impact. Even when this is the case, however, it is important not to base our total assessment of the candidate on their impact. The fact that a young lady appears charming and attractive at an interview does not automatically qualify her as a good candidate to be an airline stewardess. It is as important that she can also be patient with difficult customers, tolerate stress, conform to company regulations and be prepared to spend long periods of time away from home. The capacity of a young lady to meet these requirements may not be demonstrated by her charming manner and appealing dress!

A sales manager at a selection interviewing course once told me that he assessed candidates before they entered his office. The sales manager explained that he made his assessment as the candidate walked from the car park or street to the office reception! Just before an interview candidate was expected, the manager would watch for the candidate to arrive. If he had an air of 'determination' and 'self-confidence' in his walk, the sales manager would make a positive assessment. If not, the manager terminated the interview after five minutes. While exhibiting a confident and positive walk may be an indication of some sales attributes, it tells us nothing about the candidate's manner with customers or whether they have the interest or ability to cope with the technical knowledge required to sell the product.

Because of the fallibility of basing assessment decisions on impact, many organisations attempt to make the assessment interviews more systematic and disciplined. These have largely involved the use of firm criteria against which candidates can be evaluated, together with improved questioning techniques so that more relevant factual data can be elicited from candidates. One of the pioneering efforts in formulating criteria against which candidates could be systematically assessed was by the National Institute of Industrial Psychology in Britain. The Institute developed the 'Seven Point Plan' which contained broad headings under which a job related employee specification could be produced. These could then be used in the interview as criteria for gathering data and finally for evaluating suitability for the target job. The Seven Point Plan uses the following headings:

1. Physique, health and appearance,
    e.g. eyesight, grooming, dress, general health.
2. Attainments,
    e.g. general education, job experience.
3. General intelligence,
    e.g. general reasoning ability.
4. Special aptitudes,
    e.g. mechanical, numerical, manual dexterity.
5. Interests,
    e.g. intellectual, practical, social, physical.
6. Disposition,
    e.g. acceptability, leadership, stability, self-reliance.

7. Circumstances,
    e.g. age, dependants, mobility, work permits.

The Seven Point Plan and similar approaches to the use of criteria in the selection interview made an important contribution in helping personnel specialists and line managers to become more systematic in their approach. It provided a broad framework within which the recruiter could decide which attributes were required for performing the target job and could then collect and evaluate candidate data against these. By using the Plan, recruiters were encouraged to anticipate the types of information that would help make an assessment, thus making it possible to identify relevant subject areas for discussion and specific questions which would elicit information on these from the candidate.

By linking use of the Seven Point Plan to improve interview techniques, for instance the use of open and closed questions, avoiding leading questions, and developing rapport with the candidate, interviewers became more effective in basing selection decisions on objective data about the candidate rather than on his or her impact. Today most large companies in Britain use employee specifications and candidate assessment forms based on the early work of the National Institute of Industrial Psychology.

Despite the advances achieved, this approach has two major weaknesses which make it vulnerable to empirical scrutiny, now increasingly demanded by social pressures, trade unions and equal opportunity legislation in the United States and other countries. The first concerns the translation of the job description into the employee specification. Traditional job descriptions frequently describe a job in terms of duties rather than job outputs, and even then rarely translate these into the behaviours required by the employee in order to achieve these outputs. With the Seven Point Plan the recruiter is required to translate the job description into the employee specification on the basis of intuition and experience. Consequently many recruitment campaigns commence with an employee specification of dubious validity. While it may be justified to state that a nursing qualification is necessary for a company nurse, it may not be necessary that new salesmen recruits have all had previous selling experience, or that a line manager has necessarily had production experience. Many requirements listed in employee specifications are open to challenge because they are not based on an objective analysis of what the job holder actually has to do to achieve the job outputs required, i.e. job behaviour.

The other fundamental weakness of this approach lies in the gathering and interpreting of information about the candidate so that a selection decision can be made. What kind of information will enable us to decide that the candidate meets the attainments, aptitudes, or disposition required in the employee specification? How do we establish that the candidate does have the leadership skills required, or that they can influence senior management? One assumption frequently made by recruiters is that the candidate needs to have performed the same or a very similar job previously in order to be effective in the target job. This is an unrealistic basis on which to make assessment, as a job in one organisation may differ substantially from a job with the same title in another.

When employees change jobs they frequently seek more challenge or variety in the new job and it is therefore unrealistic to look for someone who has performed exactly the same job before. A production manager in charge of 250 employees will usually want his next job to have greater staff responsibility; a management accountant is likely to seek a more responsible finance position in his next job rather than a similar management accountant's job. Increased employee expectations as well as rapidly changing technology in all spheres of business make it increasingly unlikely that recruiters can expect to take on candidates who have performed the same job in another organisation. This makes it even more essential that an effective vehicle is provided for recruiters to identify in precise terms whether candidates possess the attributes required for success in the job to be filled. Failure to confront this issue can only result in inappropriate selection decisions.

THE BEHAVIOUR TECHNOLOGY METHOD OF SELECTION INTERVIEWING

Two major requirements to improve the effectiveness of selection interviews are defined job performance requirements which specify the behaviours required for success, and an interview strategy which makes it possible to obtain behavioural information from the candidate which can then be compared to job behaviour requirements. The previous chapter described an approach to defining both the problem-solving and emotional behaviours required to achieve the outputs of a job, and this requirement therefore needs little discussion. The outstanding problem is how to obtain behavioural data about the candidate in the interview so that this can be matched against requirements.

One of the conclusions of much psychological research is that once we are grown up (twenty-five years plus) our behaviour patterns tend to be relatively stable. While there are exceptions to this, the weight of evidence suggests that our capacity for change is fairly small. While we can all probably point to an individual whose job performance has undergone significant changes (for better or worse) over a period of time, this is often due to the fact that the individual's work situation has changed. While one environment may stifle a particularly creative individual, a different job, company or work environment may enable them to blossom to an unexpected degree. Working for a manager who sets overall objectives may allow an independent individual to use his talents to the full, while the same employee reporting to a manager who does not delegate responsibility but only prescribes tasks may produce a much lower standard of performance. It therefore follows that one of the best predictors of individual performance in a job is to identify individual behaviour and performance in past situations which were similar to those found in the target job. If we want to identify a candidate's ability to lead a group of subordinates, we need to identify what that person did in previous group situations. Information about past behaviour in meetings is likely to be a useful predictor of behaviour in future meetings. Equally, if a job requires a very high level of problem analysis and judgement we would look to the candidate's behaviour in previous job situations where high levels of problem analysis were required.

Emotional behaviour is similarly stable. If a job requires close supervision of subordinates, it may be necessary as part of the defined job performance requirements that the candidate can use his Critical and Nurturing Parent ego states. Interview questions could therefore be directed to identify whether the candidate had used these ego states in their dealings with people in the past. Similarly, if a job requires developing many new relationships with people it is likely that this would require the use of Child behaviours. Once again an interview for such a job (and this often applies to sales positions) would involve identifying that person's use of Child behaviour patterns with others.

Identifying candidate behaviour patterns in the past that help us to predict future job behaviours can be achieved by various interviewing techniques. The overall approach is to encourage the candidate to talk in detail about what they did in specific past situations which resembled those in the target job. If we needed to evaluate a candidate's ability to lead a group, we might ask them to describe the meetings they attend on a regular basis. We would then probe their behaviour with specific questions such as: 'Tell me about your contribution to that meeting,' or 'How did you help the group to overcome this problem?'. To find out about groups the candidate led we might ask: 'Are there any groups/meetings in which you were the chairman?' and perhaps follow up with a question such as: 'Did you prepare an agenda for the meeting, and if so, what did it include?' or 'How did you know that everyone understood the purpose of the meeting — what did you say?'

The approach essentially involves asking candidates to recount particular incidents from their past which are similar to those expected in the target job, and to describe precisely what they did. This approach is sometimes labelled 'critical incident interviewing'. Because a candidate will have a better recall of what he or she did more recently than what they did five or ten years ago, recent critical incidents are likely to be more relevant than those from many years previously. The interviewer's objective should therefore be to concentrate on the most recent critical incidents in the candidate's past which are related to situations in the target job.

During the interview, the specific responses of the candidate are recorded. After the interview, the data is classified against the problem-solving and TA behaviour categories. The important benefit of this approach is that it makes possible the collection of specific behaviour information, which, after the interview, can be related to the behaviour required in the job.

During the interview the assessor has more than enough to concentrate on in asking relevant questions and recording the answers. Attempting at the same time to evaluate candidate responses against TA and the Problem-Solving Dimensions would create interviewer overload. The results of using the two step approach of separating the collection and recording of information from its evaluation have surprised many interviewers. Whereas an interviewer may have a positive impression of the candidate from their initial impact during the interview, later review of the behavioural data gathered may show that the candidate clearly does not meet the required specification. Interviewers who start using this approach find the contrast particularly noticeable. Only when we separate the process of collecting data from its evaluation are we likely to make an objective and impartial assessment, based more on actual evidence than personal reactions.

Rather than describe the theory of this approach further, it might be more helpful to consider a specific example of behaviour collected from a critical incident job interview. The interview described below was for selection of a personnel manager. One performance requirement of this role was responsiveness to the needs of line management which in terms of Problem-Solving Dimensions was seen to be sensitivity, adaptability and planning, and in TA terms was a requirement for use of the Adapted Child and Adult ego states. Another performance requirement of this role was administrative ability. This was seen in Problem-Solving Dimensions terms as attention to detail, planning and organising, problem analysis and management control, while from a TA perspective it was seen as a well developed Critical Parent and Adult. Before reading the evaluation of the data collected, make your own assessment of the candidate in terms of these requirements.

Interviewer: Tell me about your last job as personnel officer.
Candidate: It covered most aspects of personnel, and particularly recruitment, training, some industrial relations and job analysis.
Interviewer: What sort of recruitment campaigns did you handle?
Candidate: Oh, these were mostly for engineers, and I ran a series of selection events to recruit engineers to go into remote branches of the business.

Interviewer: How effective were these events?

Candidate: In the end, I got them running quite well and had them running on a routine basis. Mostly each event would result in the appointment of three or four engineers, and we were able to make up for the turnover of engineers from the business. The point was that we were able to recruit engineers at half the fee an agency would charge, so it must have been effective.

Interviewer: That's interesting. On what basis did you work that out?

Candidate: Well, actually it was an estimate. It just seemed that the costs were half what they would otherwise have been.

Interviewer: So there was a running tally kept of recruitment costs?

Candidate: Ah, well, I suppose not, but no one complained about costs so I assumed that it must have been all right.

Interviewer: Let's move on to the way you assessed candidates. Tell me something about how you did this.

Candidate: I assessed candidates on the basis of an interview and three psychological tests, a verbal, quantitative, and electronic thinking test. After some time, it seemed that the electronic test was not very useful in predicting success, so I withdrew it. Combined, the other tests seemed to give a good indication of success and we had only a low drop-out rate of those I selected in the first year.

Interviewer: That sounds useful. Who actually carried out this validation study, and how?

Candidate: I suggested that it should be carried out and one of our corporate recruitment consultants undertook the exercise. I'm not really sure how he did it exactly, but his report was comprehensive and it made a good impression on line managers who were recruiting engineers.

Interviewer: When you said you suggested it should be carried out, who did you put the idea to and why?

Candidate: Well, I realised that I was spending a lot of my time on recruitment, and when I was talking to one of the line managers he mentioned that such a study had been undertaken for graduates, so I contacted central recruitment and asked them if they could do the same sort of thing for engineers.

Interviewer: Let's move on. What sort of administrative systems did you use in the recruitment campaigns?

Candidate: The usual thing, recording of candidates responding to enquiries, offers being made, and my secretary did all of that.

Interviewer: It's often difficult to get line managers to operate personnel systems and administrative routines. Give me an example of how you dealt with a manager who was not operating one of your systems correctly.

Candidate: Well, administration is a drag. Mind you, I know I have to do

it so I get on with it. My view is that we all have to do administration,
everyone has to stick to the regulations. As long as that happens, there
are no problems.

Interviewer: Yes, but what have you done when a manager has not
adhered to the regulations?

Candidate: Well, last week, a manager hadn't got authorisation to recruit,
but I got on with the recruitment campaign anyway to save messing
around.

Interviewer: What would have happened if that authorisation had not
come through?

Candidate: Oh well, we'd be in trouble, because I might have spent money
advertising and all that, and if authorisation hadn't been given in the
end it would all have been rather embarrassing.

Interviewer: Have you ever started a campaign and later found that
authorisation was not forthcoming?

Candidate: Well, it's happened a few times, but I always get on with
things when a manager asks me to.

What is your assessment of this candidate under the following headings:

1. Sensitivity;
2. Adaptability;
3. Planning and organising;
4. Attention to detail;
5. Judgement and management control.

Which ego states did the candidate use and in what proportion? What
evidence do you have to support your evaluation?

While the above interchange is only a sample from an interview, it has
provided considerable information about the candidate's behaviour. From
what was said, we can draw the following conclusions:

1. *Sensitivity*
   High, as shown by the following statements: 'no one complained
   about costs, so I assumed that it must have been all right,' 'when I was
   talking to one line manager, he mentioned that such a study had been
   undertaken . . .'.

2. *Adaptability*
   High, as indicated by the following statements: 'Well, last week, a
   manager hadn't got authorisation to recruit, but I got on with the
   recruitment campaign anyway to save messing around,' 'It seemed
   that the electronic test was not very useful in predicting success, so I
   withdrew it.'

3. *Attention to detail*
   Low, as suggested by the following: 'Well, actually it was an estimate.
   It seemed that costs were half what they would otherwise have been,'

'I'm not really sure how he did it exactly, but his report was comprehensive.'

4. *Judgement*

   Mixed data indicated by the following: 'each event would result in
   the appointment of three or four engineers, and we were able to make
   up for the turnover of engineers from the business,' which is a positive
   indication. 'Oh well, we'd be in trouble, because I may have spent
   money advertising . . . Well, it's happened a few times, but I always
   get on with things when a manager asks me to.' This is an example of
   poor judgement and shows that the candidate had not learned from
   his experience of what happens when he starts a recruitment campaign
   without authority to recruit.

5. *Management control*

   Low to medium as supported by the following: 'Ah, well, I suppose
   not, but no one complained about costs so I assumed that it must
   have been all right,' which is an example of awareness of the fact that
   the organisation paid little attention to costs, but also reflects no
   attempt to do anything to evaluate and control costs. 'It seemed that
   the electronic test was not very useful in predicting success, so I withdrew it,' is an example of exercising positive control. 'Well, last week,
   a manager hadn't got authorisation to recruit, but I got on with the
   recruitment campaign anyway, is an example of low management
   control.

Although this extract from the interview is concerned with exploring the
candidate's professional skills from the point of view of the Problem-
Solving Dimensions, there is also useful data about the candidate's ego
states. In real life interviews the words used by the candidate would be
reinforced by their non-verbal communication. Nevertheless, the words
used here suggest an ego state profile. The profile shown by the above data
is a large Adapted Child, moderately developed Adult, and low Critical
Parent. There is no evidence concerning the Nurturing Parent and only one
piece of Free Child data. This is as follows:

Critical Parent: Low, e.g. only one positive indication, 'It must have been
cost effective'.

Adult: Reasonably developed, e.g. 'and we were able to make up
                  for the turnover of engineers', and negatively, 'It just
                  seemed that the costs were half what they would other-
                  wise have been.' This example is apparently rational
                  assessment, but is in fact a Critical Parent judgement, not
                  based on evidence. Another positive indication is when
                  the candidate said: 'Combined, the other tests gave a good
                  indication of success, and we had only a low drop-out rate
                  of those I selected in the first year.'

Adapted Child: There is considerable data which suggests that the candidate has a well developed Adapted Child: 'Ah, well, I
suppose not, but no one complained about costs', and
later about administration: 'Mind you, I know I have to
do it', and later still, 'I always get on with things when a
manager asks me to.'

Free Child: The question responses provide relatively little opportunity for expression of the Free Child, and the only
example is 'administration is a drag'.

Taking this data, we are in a position to make some assessment of the
candidate's suitability against the criteria originally specified. From the
point of view of the Problem-Solving Dimensions, he has high sensitivity
and adaptability, and low attention to detail and management control,
and mixed data on judgement. The candidate has, from the discussion, a
well developed Adapted Child, and there is little information on Free
Child and none on Nurturing Parent. Overall, therefore, the candidate
would appear from the available data not to meet the specification
perfectly.

This chapter has shown the difficulties inherent in the conventional
approach of assessment interviews. Despite these drawbacks, however, it is
practicable to obtain a lot a high quality behavioural information about
a candidate which can be matched to an existing specification. By using
appropriate questions we can identify information from critical incidents
in the past experience of the candidate which suggest the types of
behaviour adopted. Used in this way, Behaviour Technology can considerably improve the effectiveness of the interview.

6 Performance appraisal and improvement

Improving individual job performance has for long been considered an objective of the appraisal systems operated by many companies. Close inspection of the paperwork associated with these systems, particularly after completion, suggests however that this objective is seldom achieved. The most concrete output of an appraisal is often a recommendation that the employee concerned should go on a training course, yet much of the research into what actually helps managers to develop suggests that training courses come low down on the list of factors which contribute to managerial success. Even the more sophisticated appraisal systems, based on concepts such as management by objectives, seem, after an initial fanfare of enthusiasm, to contribute little to improved job and business performance.

This chapter reviews some of the issues in performance appraisal and improvement, and goes on to describe a performance improvement system recently installed in International Computers Limited based on Behaviour Technology.

THE FUNCTIONS OF APPRAISAL

While the objectives of some appraisal schemes are clearly stated, those of others tend to get lost in the mass of paperwork that surrounds the completion of pre-appraisal forms, appraisal forms, job improvement plans, career plans and the rest. Appraisal systems can serve three possible objectives: a reward review, a review of performance and an assessment of potential.[1] A reward review is the mechanism by which a boss informs his subordinate about the changes he has been given in pay, responsibility, etc. as a result of his performance. This review is frequently based on some form of assessment which the manager makes of the subordinate, which is then used to justify the change in rewards that have been allocated. A performance review is the evaluation of a subordinate's job performance and achievements. While in some cases this assessment may be an end in itself, in other systems there is a definite attempt to use this as a basis for improving future performance by formulating job improvement plans based on an identified performance gap. A further possible objective of appraisal systems is to evaluate future potential in terms of the next job or career stream for which an individual is considered or for long-term potential to reach senior echelons in the organisation.

In addition to these three formal objectives, an appraisal will inevitably be moulded by the individual manager conducting it to suit his own style of management. The authoritarian Critical Parent boss may well adapt the appraisal system to put down his subordinates so that all their development needs are carefully exposed, while their strengths are ignored. At the other extreme, the laissez-faire type of boss or 'loner' may leave subordinates to do the whole appraisal themselves, and never provide any feedback either positive or negative. These two types of management approach to the appraisal would be derived respectively from managers with a large Critical Parent and a large Adapted Child.

The objectives served by an appraisal system will also, in practice, be related to the business climate in which the organisation operates, as well as the company management style. A company experiencing very high growth rates may well need to pay most attention to managers' potential to fill future positions that will arise. In contrast to this, a company confronted with increasing competition in the market place, or a contracting market, is likely to need to pay particular attention to improving the performance of employees in their existing positions. Organisations with monopolistic dominance of a market and with little likelihood of threat may be inclined to ignore both of these two objectives, and use the appraisal system mainly for allocating rewards to employees. Organisations with a highly authoritarian management style will tend to operate dictatorial appraisal systems while those which value complex problem-solving will tend to have highly elaborate appraisal systems.

To put forward a single method of performance appraisal which would be suitable for all organisations would clearly be unrealistic. Inevitably, the appraisal system operated by an organisation will need to take account of its business requirements as well as its dominant management style. This chapter will therefore concentrate on appraisal processes which have as their primary objective the improvement of present job performance of employees. While other objectives may be valid for particular organisations, these will not be considered. See Chapter 10 for the assessment of potential.

THE TRADITIONAL PERFORMANCE APPRAISAL

Traditional appraisal processes in many organisations consist of an assessment made by the manager and an interview during which this is fed back to the employee with suggestions on where he or she needs to improve. While this form of appraisal is obviously better than no appraisal or feedback at all, it has a number of serious drawbacks. The most fundamental is that the manager frequently forms his assessment independently and takes very little account of the subordinate's views about their own performance and the problems they were facing. Typically, superiors may identify weaknesses or failings in their staff but be oblivious to the factors which create difficulties for them. This results in the manager telling the employee what was wrong with him, and gaining little or no commitment to change. Even if the manager makes an accurate analysis of the subordinate's performance shortcomings, this approach is unlikely to encourage the subordinate to accept the analysis or to want to do anything to improve. The ultimate cliché example of this type of appraisal is the one carried out when the boss encounters the subordinate in the lift.

Boss: Things seem to have gone quite well this year, don't they?
Subordinate: Yes, not bad at all.
Boss: Do tighten up on the stock control this year though, won't you?
    Right, keep up the good work.

The lift arrives at the next floor and the boss leaves. While this archetypal example of an appraisal is an exaggeration, it does happen that managers claim they have carried out face to face appraisal interviews with their subordinates, while the subordinate is completely unaware that this has occurred!

The most fundamental requirement of an effective appraisal system is that the subordinate needs to be involved in the process, both in the assessment of performance as well as in the action designed to improve future performance. Without real involvement, the subordinate is unlikely either to accept the appraisal or agree to follow-up action.

Another drawback of conventional appraisal mechanisms is that they involve assessment on a single list of employee traits or characteristics. Typical traits might be: disposition, appearance, drive, business understanding. On the surface these may seem relevant dimensions on which to assess a manager, but closer inspection will show how inadequate they are. These labels suffer from three basic difficulties.

The first difficulty with dimensions such as 'drive' or 'disposition' is that they are difficult to define. Is 'drive' a reference to initiative, energy or assertiveness or is it some vague indication of 'management virility'? Terms such as 'drive' or 'disposition' are vague and ill-defined. What one person may regard as high drive may be seen as pushy by another or as flash by a third. To be of value, the dimensions on which employees are assessed need to be definable and recognisable.

Another difficulty with these terms is that they tend to describe what a person is rather than what a person does. If you tell me that I have no 'drive' or that I have a poor 'disposition', this labels what I am, and by definitition this is very difficult for me to change. On the other hand, if you tell me that I do not take as much initiative as I could, this is a comment about what I do. The distinction is more than a quibble; it is a fundamental issue which affects our ability to change, for I am more likely to be able to control and change what I do than what I am. So a further requirement for an appraisal system is that it should assess what a person does (and has control over) rather than what a person is (which is fixed). Appraisal quite simply needs to concentrate on behaviour and outputs rather than on personality traits.

The third difficulty with many appraisal systems is that they use the same dimensions for assessing all employees. While it may be essential that a salesman show plenty of 'initiative' or use a lot of the Free Child with his customers, this may be inappropriate behaviour for a clerical supervisor. In fact, if a clerical supervisor demonstrated high initiative this would be dysfunctional for many organisations, as this type of role typically requires an employee who can operate a well defined system rather than someone who can suggest improvements or get round the system. Other typically standardised assessment criteria yardsticks are timekeeping or appearance. While timekeeping may be important in jobs where the incumbant sets standards for others, it may be unimportant in other jobs. Appearance equally may be important for someone who is representing the company to the outside world, but it is unlikely to be of consequence in computer departments which work in isolation from others and where most interaction is mainly between members of the department.

APPRAISAL OF PERFORMANCE AND BEHAVIOUR

Making appraisal criteria job-related is a prerequisite if the process is to lead to actions by the job holder and the boss to improve performance. Assessment against abstract and irrelevant criteria fulfils no constructive function, apart from perpetuating values which individuals who designed the appraisal system believed were important. The need is to assess performance against the previously agreed performance objectives, and then examine the behaviour of the job holder in terms of whether it did or did not contribute to their achievement. Ideally, this would be based on a careful definition of job performance requirements as proposed in Chapter 4. However, this may not be practicable for all jobs in the organisation, and therefore the appraisal system will need to encourage the boss and job holder jointly to identify and agree on those behaviours which contribute most to achievement of performance outcomes. (A method of achieving this will be considered later in the chapter.) Only when boss and subordinate agree behaviour criteria which determine job performance will they be able to evaluate actual behaviours by the job holder which contributed to or detracted from the level of outcomes achieved. This will then make it possible to identify shortcomings in performance so that the job holder can concentrate on the specific behaviours which will most improve future performance.

This may seem like a double appraisal process. However, this is precisely what is required if appraisal is to lead to performance improvement. The first step involves an assessment of individual achievement of job outputs (which should have been previously agreed between boss and subordinate). Only after this has been done is it meaningful to consider the behaviours of the job holder that contributed to these outcomes. Most appraisal systems fail to undertake this second stage. Consequently, even when performance shortcomings are identified, e.g. 'sales were below the level targeted', or 'training courses fail to obtain the level of participant satisfaction specified', it becomes difficult to identify and overcome the reasons for this.

Failure of a training course to obtain the level of participant satisfaction required could be due to a variety of reasons. It might be due to a lack of planning of the course content, or failure to organise the event effectively at the time. Alternatively, it might be that the trainer failed to develop sufficient rapport with course members due to a lack of Nurturing Parent or Free Child behaviours. Yet another explanation is that the selection process for course members encouraged inappropriate individuals to attend the programme, due to a lack of Critical Parent and/or management control by the trainer. These and other possible reasons may be why course members' ratings were lower than required. Only by examining the behaviour of the trainer will it be possible to identify with precision what he or she did or did not do which led to participant satisfaction ratings below the level required. After such an analysis has been carried out, it will then be possible for both the job holder and boss to formulate and agree an action plan which will contribute directly to improving the identified performance shortcomings.

Management by objectives achieved considerable acclaim during the 1970s as a useful method of improving individual and in turn organisational effectiveness. It focused manager's attention on the importance of clarifying what they were trying to achieve, so that they could direct their energies towards important results rather than trivial ones. In many organisations, this approach has not lived up to its expectations for improving performance. When achievements were reviewed against objectives, MBO systems provided clear yardsticks against which individual performance could be assessed. Unfortunately, such systems seldom enabled either the boss or the job holder to come to grips with the real causes of under or over-achievement of objectives set.

While assessment of performance against job objectives can provide many benefits, when this occurs without consideration of employee behaviour it provides little basis for improving future performance. Consequently, if overall objectives remain largely the same (as they tend to do for managers who do not change jobs) operation of an MBO system proves to have little long-term benefit for the individual, apart from identifying overall performance problem areas. The knowledge that we have failed to achieve a particular objective serves little practical purpose apart from becoming a potential cause of frustration. To improve our performance it is necessary that we know exactly what it is we do inappropriately.

Only when the specific behaviour deficiency which brought about a performance shortcoming is identified can the job holder and boss agree a meaningful action plan to improve performance. If, as in the earlier example, it was agreed that the reason for low training course participant ratings was due to poor preparation and planning for the course, the boss and subordinate might agree that steps would be taken within certain timescales before future courses are due to run, e.g. the complete course programme would be prepared one week before the event, with detailed objectives for each session, which the trainer would submit to his boss as an example of increased planning and organising behaviour. Alternatively, it might be agreed that the subordinate discuss and review his notes for new sessions with a colleague, or that he work side by side with another trainer who is known to be effective in planning and preparing for courses.

If the reason for poor training course evaluations by members is agreed to be that the trainer did not develop sufficiently close relationships with them, due to a lack of Nurturing Parent (i.e. taking care of/sympathising with course members' problems), a totally different plan would be required. One option might be to develop the trainer's sensitivity to the impact of his own behaviour on others by attending an interpersonal skills development programme. A more practical step might be for the trainer to anticipate the problems and difficulties that course members might face during the programme. This would enable him to include reference to these issues within the course.

Alternatively, the trainer may need to organise more time for the course to work in small groups and spend time with each small group in tackling their problems. If the poor relationships with course members were due to a lack of spontaneity, a different approach would be needed. One option might be for the trainer to practice sharing his feelings during the programme, e.g. by letting participants know that the trainer himself has difficulty in grappling with the issues raised on the programme, or by sharing his or her own pleasure and interest in the subject under discussion. The trainer might then have a colleague sitting in on a course he is running with a view to giving feedback on his practice of using Nurturing Parent or Free Child behaviours.

Any performance shortfall can be attributable to a number of possible individual behaviours, so unless the precise behavioural deficiencies are identified it is impossible to attempt to improve performance. If, as has been argued, precise job objectives cannot be determined, then it will come as no surprise that the job holder's performance is unsatisfactory! Worse still any attempt at appraising performance becomes laughable, as the activity will be entirely dependent on the assessor who undertakes it. While it is wholly appropriate that the evaluation of beauty should lie in the eye of the beholder, the evaluation of employee performance needs to be undertaken on a more substantial basis than the whim of the assessor if it is to have value for business performance.

If improving employee performance is an organisation priority, this cannot be reduced to a once a year activity. Many experts in this area advocate that the annual formal performance appraisal discussion concerned with improving current performance should contain no surprises. Rather, it should bring together a number of issues which have already been discussed between boss and subordinate. In some organisations appraisals take place every three months to tackle short-term performance, while in others the ongoing dialogue between boss and subordinate on a daily basis is the main vehicle for improvement in performance, with the yearly formal appraisal serving merely as an opportunity to put together all the issues raised during the previous twelve months. No single method will suit all organisations or business environments. The one point that can be made with confidence is that any appraisal mechanism which is exclusively an annual activity is unlikely to contribute much to organisation effectiveness. Action plans agreed at an appraisal need to be monitored to ensure that they are being implemented. Objectives may need to be changed to meet changed business circumstances. While some companies undoubtedly do treat appraisal as a once a year activity, this is likely to be carried out solely to meet an enforced personnel regulation or a line management edict.

THE INTERNATIONAL COMPUTERS LIMITED
UK DIVISION APPRAISAL SYSTEM

Performance appraisal became an established management discipline in the UK Division of ICL during the 1970s. By 1980, however, a number of problems had been encountered in the operation of the system by both line management and personnel. The complaint from line management was that the whole system had become unduly bureaucratic, involving the completion of many forms. Even when completed, the various pieces of paper appeared to have little consequence, and therefore line managers were, understandably, reluctant to indulge in what had become a paper dominated exercise, rather than a practical tool which assisted them in achieving business objectives.

Another drawback was the use of a fixed number of criteria for the assessment of all employees. The use of assessment centres had already demonstrated that different business needs and management styles across the country created different behaviour requirements on holders of the same type of job in different locations. While high levels of planning and organisation were a major requirement of sales managers in large computer mainframe markets, it was far less important for sales managers concerned with selling computers to first time users. The system of performance appraisal imposed a set of criteria for evaluating management behaviour which from experience was not totally relevant to any one type of job, let alone to different jobs.

From a personnel perspective, the performance appraisal system had further disadvantages. One was that although the system used management behaviour criteria for assessment of performance, these differed from the set of widely used criteria for assessing performance in assessment centres. The assessment centre evaluations were the Problem-Solving Dimensions described in Chapter 2, but these were not used in the performance appraisal system. In view of the widespread understanding of the Problem-Solving Dimensions among managers as a result of involvement both as assessors and candidates on assessment centres, it seemed a pity that these same dimensions were not also used in the performance appraisal.

A final difficulty with the performance appraisal system was that it appeared to emphasise future career moves rather than improving existing job performance. Even though the impact of the recession on the company was, at that time, just beginning to be felt, it was apparent to many of us in management development at the time that more emphasis would need to be placed on improving current job performance, rather than on the assessment of future potential. The later manpower reduction exercises of 1981 and 1982 demonstrated how important this change of emphasis was.

As a result of these shortcomings, a new appraisal system was introduced into the division in 1980. Besides correcting the identified shortcomings, the new appraisal system had three stated objectives of which the improvement of employee current job performance, through the joint efforts of boss and subordinate, was the most important. After preparation by both parties, the new appraisal system involved three stages:

1. *Achievement report*
    This involves an assessment of the job holder's achievement against objectives set the previous year. It concerns the outcomes achieved by the job holder, and as far as practicable is based on facts as opposed to opinions. It is common practice in the company to specify objectives, usually in quantitative terms. This is easy for sales jobs, e.g. revenue, orders placed, and proportion of repeat business, but quantitative measures can also be determined for other jobs, e.g. personnel. Someone involved in recruitment may have specified financial targets set

for the cost of campaigns, or timescales for filling vacancies. A management development specialist may have a target for number of completed appraisals (!), budgets for training, numbers and quality standards for assessment centres, etc.

2.   *Review of personal performance*
This part of the appraisal looks at the job holder's behaviour in terms of the Problem-Solving Dimensions given earlier. Most managers had already used the Problem-Solving Dimensions in assessment centres which are used for promotion to first and second line management (i.e. first appointment as a manager in charge of a group, or second line management as a manager in charge of other managers). Managers and subordinates select the six most important Problem-Solving Dimensions they consider to contribute to achievement of the job holder's objectives, and assess behaviour against these. Managers already had available lists of dimensions which were in use for assessment centre evaluations for specific jobs and could use these. Alternatively, they could select different dimensions if they considered this appropriate. This flexible approach enabled boss and subordinate to review behaviour against the unique requirements of the subordinate's job. During the appraisal discussion, the subordinate's behaviour was assessed against the chosen dimension. By agreeing the Problem-Solving Dimensions beforehand, both boss and subordinate were ensuring that they were assessing the same aspects of job behaviour, something which does not always happen.

Because of widespread involvement in assessment centres, managers in the division already had a good grasp of the types of behaviours which fall into each Problem-Solving Dimension. Without some experience in using the dimensions, it would not have been practicable to introduce their use without training for the managers concerned.

3   *Job improvement plan*
The third part of the appraisal process involves formulation of a job improvement plan. This involves planning action steps to be taken by both boss and subordinate which will improve subordinate behaviour in the three or four dimensions where improvement is most required. Apart from the conventional favourites of training courses, these could involve more regular reviews of critical job situations, working with colleagues to solve particular problems, or practice in particular aspects of the job for development purposes. The appraisal is not considered appropriate for setting up new job objectives, but rather as a mechanism to improve performance of the job holder. A separate discussion may well occur for the revision and updating of job objectives.

Extracts from the appraisal form currently in use can be found on pages 93 to 96.

United
Kingdom
Division

Staff
restricted

Management
and professional
staff

Appraisal

This form should be completed only after reference to the Performance Appraisal Notes.

Annual	Obligatory	Interim	
Name			Personal no.
Job title			Date of birth
SS/Grade			Date joined company
Building code			Date of appointment to present job
Sector/Region			Date of last appraisal
Area/Project			Date of interview
Appraiser			

Achievement report

Summarise the results achieved by the Job Holder as compared with those expected of him and known to him, e.g. in the Job Description and current objectives.

Objectives	Achievements

Add continuation sheets if required.

2   Review of personal performance

Identify the six most important attributes for effective job performance, e.g. planning and organising, leadership, technical skills (a list of possible attributes is given in the appraisal notes)   nd evaluate strengths and weaknesses with actual examples, in the light of the results achieved.

a.   ___________________________________

b.   ___________________________________

c.   ___________________________________

d.   ___________________________________

e.   ___________________________________

f.   ___________________________________

g.   Any other factors which have influenced performance.

---

3   Overall performance assessment

Overall performance rating:

See appraisal notes for scale to be used

6   Career development

What are the main strengths/development needs relevant to the individual's career development?

What plans are there if appropriate to increase the responsibilities in the present job?

What is the most likely next job/career stream for the individual? When is this likely to occur—within 1 year, between 1 and 2 years or after 2 years? Identify separate plans if appropriate for within and outside UKD. Specify any actions required and by whom to achieve these recommendations.

Within UKD

Outside UKD

Are there any constraints, including mobility?

Is attendance of an assessment centre/panel required within 12 months to pursue these career objectives?

Type

Timing

7   Reviewing manager's comments on performance plus potential

| Reviewing manager's signature | Name in capitals | Date |

The appraisal system also serves reward and future career functions, but these are considered secondary to the main objective of improving current job performance.

Reactions from line management to the new appraisal system were highly favourable. The fact that it reduced the paperwork by over half created a positive response in itself. More importantly the flexibility of the approach enabled individuals to be appraised against only those behaviours which mattered in their jobs. In consequence, the job improvement plans generated tended to be more realistic and constructive. Perhaps the acid test of its success is that the system was subsequently applied to other groups of staff, for instance engineering managers.

REFERENCE

1) Randall, G.A., Packard, P.M.A., Shaw, R.L., and Slater, A.J., *Staff Appraisal*, Institute of Personnel Management, 1972.

7 Working in groups

The importance of groups in business is widely recognised by managers, many of whom spend a significant proportion of their working time in groups of one type or another. Whereas committees or department meetings were once the predominant type of work group, new forms of work group have become increasingly common such as 'project teams' or 'task forces'. As well as conferring a special status, these new types of groups illustrate that in addition to controlling and managing existing operations, groups can play a key role in spearheading and implementing changes. Whereas the traditional committee or department meeting is frequently seen as an established entity which will continue for many years, the new forms of groups are frequently shortlived. They are set up to achieve some specific objective, which once attained leads to dissolution of the group.

The role of the work group in organisations has not escaped the attention of either industrial psychologists or organisation experts. A body of research literature has been built up over the last fifty years which makes this area second only to motivation in importance as a feature of organisational life to be investigated. Much of this research has centred on a central concern of Behaviour Technology; the behaviour of individuals in a group. By looking at behaviour, academics have been able to shed useful light on the ways in which groups function. This chapter reviews some of these findings and places them within the framework used for understanding behaviour, namely the Problem-Solving Dimensions and the TA ego states.

First we might consider the issue of definition. Many different definitions of groups can be found in the literature. Two very different ones interestingly lead to the same practical conclusion; one of them is that a work group is a number of people who meet face to face and share common (work) objectives, and another less behavioural definition[1] is that a group is a collection of people who perceive themselves to be a group. While five individuals waiting at a bus stop in silence may not constitute a group, if the bus is overdue there is a likelihood that they may start talking about their predicament and perhaps discuss the alternative courses of action open to them to achieve their objectives, for instance could they share a taxi? Once in discussion, the five individuals at the bus stop will quickly become aware that they are a group, while also having fulfilled the other definition by interacting face to face with a shared objective.

THE EARLY RESEARCH INTO GROUPS

The impetus to much of the later work into groups stemmed from research at the General Electric Hawthorne Works in the early 1930s.[2] One report, referred to as the 'Relay Test Assembly Room Study', forced social scientists to the important conclusion that the social and emotional conditions in a group can make more impact on output and performance than such physical factors as the lighting or the length of break times. The study was originally set up to investigate the effect of altering lighting conditions on the output of the girls in the Relay Test Assembly Room. Each time the experimenters changed conditions, production increased substantially. However, when the original poorly lit conditions prior to the experiment were reintroduced, output increased yet again, thus conclusively demonstrating that lighting and break times were not the causes of increased output. Closer investigation showed that the increased output was largely due to higher morale among the girls, brought about by their feelings of importance in being singled out for the experiment, and the improved relations that developed between them and their supervisor. In TA terms, this led to increased Free Child behaviour which provided energy for their Adult to get on with work and undertake problem analysis and other problem-solving behaviours.

After the unexpected results of this study, a further investigation into group behaviour was set up in the Bank Wiring Observation Room. This was concerned with the interaction (transactions) of members of this work group and involved observation and recording of individual and collective behaviour by a researcher who was present in the work room. After initial suspicion and resentment the researcher's presence was accepted and the group members continued in their previous work patterns. The most important finding of this study was the existence of rules of behaviour or norms. These concerned the task activities of the group, e.g. what constituted a fair day's work and how it should be done, as well as social relationships involving the playing of games and the formation of friendship cliques. Transgression of either work or social rules by any member of the group usually led to pressure from other group members until that individual modified his behaviour in accordance with the rules.

In TA terms rules formed the collective Critical Parent of the group. Any member who broke the rules would receive a series of Critical Parent behaviours from the others, e.g. someone who produced more than the group output norm was called a 'rate-buster' while someone who told a supervisor anything to the detriment of an associate was labelled a 'squealer'. The importance of this investigation is that it demonstrated in clear terms the way in which work behaviour (use of the Adult ego state and problem analysis) was significantly influenced by informal rules, and how these were enforced by the Critical Parent of other group members.

Research in the early 1950s investigated work group behaviour with quantitative ratings of what people did. An important development by Bales and his associates[3] was the creation of a framework — the Interaction Matrix — for categorising and analysing group behaviour. This covered both task and emotional behaviours, and could be used by observers to understand the types of interactions which occurred in a group. The categories developed by Bales are:

Positive reactions:
   (a) Shows solidarity
   (b) Shows tension release
   (c) Shows agreement
Attempted problem-solving:
   (d) Gives suggestion
   (e) Gives opinion
   (f) Gives orientation
Questions:
   (g) Asks orientation
   (h) Asks opinion
   (i) Asks suggestion
Negative reactions:
   (j) Shows disagreement
   (k) Shows tension increase
   (l) Shows antagonism

This framework can be regarded as one of the first examples of Behaviour Technology. Each of the twelve behaviour categories is precisely defined and can be used to evaluate a group discussion.

Using this framework, Bales and his associates made the significant discovery that two distinct roles tend to emerge as a group matures. One of these roles is the 'ideas man', who concentrates on the group task and uses predominantly the three 'attempted problem-solving' behaviours from the above list. The second role to emerge is that of the 'best liked man', who exhibits most of the three 'positive reactions' behaviours shown above. The emergence of these two different roles supports the idea that survival of any human system depends on the solution of two problems: (a) the achievement of the purposes for which the system was formed (i.e. task objectives); (b) the satisfaction of the personal, social and emotional needs of the members of the system. Unless progress is made in satisfying both of these needs, the survival of the group will be jeopardised. At work, task objectives are considered the most important. However, unless there is also a degree of satisfaction of members' personal needs, the group will eventually cease to work effectively. If we derive no satisfaction either from performing the task in hand or from our colleagues with whom we work, we will become frustrated and put less effort into our work. This is precisely what occurs when committees design racehorses in the shape of camels.

With groups that are primarily concerned with satisfying personal needs, e.g. social clubs and drinking groups, the task in hand is subservient to the satisfaction of group member needs. If a group fails to satisfy members' needs, they either leave the group or tag along, bored and indifferent to what is going on.

In theory, it might be desirable to have a single person fulfil both the 'ideas man' and 'best liked man' roles in a group. In practice, however, it is rare to find individuals with the skills necessary to be effective at both. One reason for this is the opposite nature of these two roles. Concentration on the group task will inevitably divert attention away from the personal needs of group members. In many instances, concentration on the task may fulfil the personal need of the task leader not to become entangled in responding to the needs of others. In contrast, the best liked role may be fulfilled by someone who needs to be liked by others and wants to avoid conflict and disharmony. Their need to be liked by others will, in itself, divert attention away from task activities. Because of this, the best liked individual is often different from the person who has most task ideas.

Bales' pioneering work has been followed by the development of other frameworks for analysing behaviour, including those of Rackham and Honey.[4] It has also stimulated the approach adopted here. Because the two basic dimensions proposed by Bales are so different, alternative methods of analysing them have been adopted. While many of the subsequent frameworks have tended to integrate the expression of feelings with the solving of task problems, this does not do justice to the facts of behaviour. Experience in and out of work has shown that although these two factors interact with one another to an important degree, they are nevertheless very different. Because task problem-solving behaviours are so different from emotional behaviours the two need to be viewed differently, and this is achieved here through the use of the Problem-Solving Dimensions and Transactional Analysis.

Undoubtedly, you will have sat through some meetings and emerged after lengthy discussions with the conviction that little or nothing was achieved. When this occurs it may have one of two likely causes. The group may have adopted inappropriate methods of tackling the problem in hand, e.g. there was insufficient problem analysis, planning and organising, attention to detail, management control, etc. Alternatively, the reason for ineffective performance was that the personal needs of individual group members dominated the behaviour of the group and interfered with achievement of the group task. This contamination might occur in a number of ways. One might be through the use of ego state behaviours which do not assist problem solving, for instance large amounts of Critical Parent or Free Child. This will often manifest itself in the playing of games such as Yes But or NIGYYSOB, referred to in Chapter 2. On the surface, these games may appear to be dealing with the task in hand, but in fact are directed at satisfying individual members' stroking patterns.

WORK GROUPS AND TECHNOLOGY

After the initial insights into the operation of groups, investigations took place into the impact of technology on group behaviour. Data from the British coal mines in the 1950s suggested that equipment and technology had far-reaching effects on behaviour and work output.[5] After improving mechanisation in the British coal mines, output per shift failed to achieve the productivity increases anticipated. After detailed study the roles and responsibilities of shift work groups were broadened to enable them to cope with the unpredictable nature of underground coal seams. In practice, this gave each shift work group the skills and capacity to tackle the tasks required to obtain coal, rather than only one set of skills from the mining cycle. A further result of this broadening of work group roles in the mines is that it decreased the competitiveness between work groups on different shifts and took account of the prevailing social values in the mining communities.

Application of the approach across international boundaries was later validated by adapting the principle from the British coal mines to the cotton mills of India.[6] Here, as a result of the introduction of more advanced mill technology, reporting relationships became unduly complex and interfered with the ability of supervision to achieve objectives. By introducing integrated work groups responsible for the complete production operation of a number of machines, it was possible to improve output because of the much wider roles now fulfilled by individual subordinates.

The efforts of twenty and more years ago have recently led to the evolvement of Group Technology. This was popularised through the work methods used for some time by Volvo automobile plants in Sweden. In the place of flow line assembly Volvo used small autonomous work groups to carry out the bulk of car assembly. In comparison with conventional car production lines, workers at Volvo fulfilled more complex and skilled assembly roles and were part of an identified team responsible for complete phases of the manufacturing process. While the precise benefits both for the company and its workforce are still being evaluated, the principles of Group Technology have been widely applied in manufacturing activities in many countries.

THE BENEFITS OF WORKING IN GROUPS

The implications of working in groups can be analysed with Behaviour Technology. The existence of a group of which an employee is an identified member is in itself likely to assist fulfilment of Child ego state behavioural needs. By working consistently with a small number of others, we are more likely to develop close personal relationships, have fun, and achieve other positive results for our Child ego state. Working with an established group of people is also likely to provide us with support of both a personal kind and in terms of getting the job done, and this involves us in receiving Nurturing Parent and Adult behaviours from others. The results of the Hawthorne studies demonstrated that groups also develop their own rules, both formal and informal, and enforcement of these will occur through Critical Parent behaviours, while compliance with these rules constitutes Adapted Child behaviour.

Working in groups provides many opportunities both to give and receive strokes. Whether our preference is to give or receive Parent, Adult or Child strokes, a group provides an opportunity to do this. Each group develops its own unique blend of stroking patterns and transactions, which affect both the personal satisfaction and well-being of the group members as well as achievement of its primary task. When a group is characterised by antagonism and conflict, this usually involves crossed transactions. These may take the form of crossed Parent transactions, from one person's Parent to the Child of the other, with the second person responding from their Parent to the first person's Child. Alternatively, the crossed transaction may take the form of one person using their Adult to communicate with the Adult of the other while he or she responds from either Critical Parent or rebellious Free Child. When groups are dominated by crossed transactions the stroking patterns will be negative; however, when transactions are parallel between the ego states the stroking patterns will be positive.

Group working can also have important benefits for task and problem-solving behaviours. Evidence from a number of sources suggests that groups are more effective than individuals working in isolation at tackling complex multiple-stage problems. It has been found that group outcomes, in terms of problem analysis and quality of judgement, will be higher than those of the same individuals working in isolation. Higher levels of decisiveness and risk taking are also characteristics of group working compared with the qualities exhibited by the same individuals working in isolation.

Implicit in many groups is the creation of common ground between members, in terms of shared information and objectives. This is enhanced when leadership is exercised in the group, allowing larger tasks to be subdivided between members and the particular expertise of each person to be made best use of. An important feature of groups is the extent to which activities are planned and organised. The importance of an agenda to the success of a group meeting bears this point out. Meetings where there is no defined plan or agenda frequently lapse into circular discussions which continue to cover the same ground over and over or go off the subject completely. Another problem-solving behaviour which is essential to effective group performance is that of management control. Without a chairman who pulls the discussion together, it frequently happens that the subject under discussion drifts on to topics of marginal importance to the group's objective. The process of debate may also become so entangled in details that the need to agree actions is forgotten.

A number of techniques have been developed to achieve more benefits from group working. To enhance the overall task achievement of groups, systematic problem-solving has become one widely used technique. This essentially involves tackling problems in a number of stages, so that different problem-solving behaviours will be used in sequence. These are:

Systematic problem-solving steps	*Predominant dimensions (problem-solving behaviours)*
Defining objectives	Leadership; initiative
Data collection	Problem analysis; attention to detail; adaptability; sensitivity
Selecting a course of action	Judgement; decisiveness; risk taking
Planning implementation	Planning and organising; leadership delegation
Implementation	Any or all problem-solving behaviours, depending on the course of action
Review	Management control; problem analysis; flexibility; judgement

The advantage of this approach to group working is that it ensures that all problem-solving behaviours necessary for solving a problem are used. By concentrating on specific behaviours at different stages of a problem, the group's attention is focused on those behaviours which are most relevant.

A development of systematic problem-solving is 'brainstorming', which assists creative problem-solving. The objective of brainstorming is to provide novel solutions to problems, often problems which have remained unresolved for a long time. It involves two distinct phases; one in which potential solutions are put forward, and a second in which these are evaluated. During the first stage, all group members are invited to put forward ideas on how the task to hand could be tackled. Each idea is usually written on a flip chart for all to see, one on top of another. Members are, however, not allowed to evaluate or criticise the ideas during this phase. Only when a whole series of possible solutions have been listed are the group encouraged to select the solution(s). This usually involves evaluating all the ideas put forward, one at a time.

The use of these two distinct phases separates ideas generation, namely problem analysis, flexibility, and creativity behaviours, from evaluation of these ideas. Evaluation usually involves judgement, management control, and attention to detail. In TA terms, the ideas phase involves Little Professor behaviours from the Child, while the evaluation phase involves Critical Parent and Adapted Child. The Adult will be used in both phases.

As well as enabling a separation of problem-solving behaviours, brainstorming has important benefits for the expression of feelings. A tendency which characterises groups is conformity with the opinions and ideas put forward by the leader or by high status group members. While this Adapted Child behaviour of members towards the leader may be beneficial under certain circumstances, it has the adverse effect of stifling the creativity of other group members by not allowing expression of any Critical Parent behaviour towards the leader or high status members, while conversely encouraging too much Critical Parent behaviour towards low status members. Brainstorming encourages group members to use less Adapted Child and more Little Professor and Adult behaviours. As group members are allowed only to put forward ideas during the stage of potential solution generation, they can build on one anothers' ideas in an unusual and creative way which would not be possible if more Critical Parent and Adult evaluation took place at the same time.

During the evaluation phase, group members consider a variety of possible solutions including those put forward by high and low status members of the group. Conformity pressures in many groups dictate that whatever the leader or high status members propose is agreed in preference to what lower status group members suggest, irrespective of the quality of the contribution. By separating out the process of evaluation from ideas generation groups are more able to give equal consideration to the suggestions of low status members as to those of high status members. This process therefore allows a greater degree of Adult rational problem analysis and judgement to be incorporated into the evaluation of ideas, and less Critical Parent and Adapted Child.

An additional benefit of brainstorming is that it increases the cohesiveness of the group by concentrating all the members' attention on the same problem. This heightened sense of purpose develops the Child's sense of belonging to the group, and facilitates stroking behaviour. As a result more energy is developed within the group for tackling its task.

The use of techniques such as brainstorming contrast with pure systematic problem-solving. Systematic problem-solving techniques channel the behaviours of group members into specific Problem-Solving Dimensions, so that in the course of tackling a problem appropriate behaviours can be adopted for each stage of work. Such techniques however pay little or no regard to the satisfaction of members' personal needs. The many investigations into group working since Hawthorne demonstrate that failure to pay sufficient attention to members' feelings ignores a major factor influencing effectiveness in achieving the group's task. Brainstorming has the advantage of dealing directly with the task problems of a group, while also indirectly satisfying some of the personal needs of group members.

The important conclusion to be drawn from the efforts of practising managers and academics is that effective performance depends on the use of appropriate problem-solving behaviour for achieving the task objectives of the group, as well as on the expression of feelings which further the aim by satisfying group members' personal needs. Failure either to use appropriate Problem-Solving Dimensions or to allow expression of feelings will prevent the group from being as effective as it might otherwise be. As yet, there is no formula available which specifies what the appropriate blend of these two types of behaviours should be. The problem-solving behaviours required will be dictated by the nature of the task being tackled by the group and the formal and informal procedures, technology and rules within the organisation. Equally the expression of feelings will depend on the individuals who make up the group, as well as on the norms that apply to the group itself and to the society in which it operates. Inevitably, there will be an interaction between these forces. If group members find the task they are tackling particularly difficult and frustrating, this will give rise to expression of feelings which adversely affect their problem-solving behaviours. In contrast, if a group finds itself to be highly successful at its prime task and is stroked by the wider organisation for its achievement, this will give rise to expression of feelings within the group which will assist it to tackle more difficult and complex tasks.

THE TEAM ROLE MODEL

With a view to maximising group performance, researchers in Britain have recently developed a framework for categorising group behaviour. This approach, known as the Team Role Model,[7] suggests that effective group performance of complex management tasks depends on the use of seven behaviour patterns within a group. These behaviour patterns involve a mixture of problem-solving behaviours and expression of feelings, as described in Table 7.1.

Table 7.1
THE TEAM ROLE MODEL

CO-ORDINATOR
The Co-ordinator organises, co-ordinates and controls the activities of the group. This involves the clarification of group objectives and problems, assigning tasks and responsibilities and encouraging group members to get involved in achieving objectives and goals. Performance of this role requires self-control, decisiveness and trust.

IDEAS MAN
The Ideas Man is concerned with putting forward ideas and strategies for achieving the objectives adopted by the group. Performance of this role requires creativity, intelligence, imagination and innovation.

CRITIC
This role involves analysing ideas and proposals being considered by the team in order to evaluate their feasibility and value for achieving the group's objectives. It is important for the Critic to point out, in a constructive manner, the weaknesses of proposals being considered. Performance of this role requires intelligence and a serious and shrewd outlook.

IMPLEMENTER
The Implementer role is concerned with the practical translation and application of concepts and plans developed by the group. This entails a down to earth outlook, coupled with perseverance in the face of difficulties. Successful performance of this role requires a practical, conventional and controlled outlook.

TEAM BUILDER
Creating and maintaining a team spirit is the main function of the Team Builder. This involves improving communications by providing personal support and warmth to group members and by overcoming tension and conflict. One needs to be socially aware and understanding to fulfil this role.

EXTERNAL CONTACT
This role involves exploring the environment outside the group by identifying ideas, information and resources. Performance of this role involves developing contacts, and co-ordination and negotiation with other groups and individuals. A stable, extrovert and inquisitive outlook is necessary to perform this role.

INSPECTOR
The Inspector ensures that the group's efforts achieve appropriate standards and that mistakes both of commission and omission are avoided. It also involves searching for failings and maintaining a sense of urgency within the group. Fulfilment of this role requires an anxious, meticulous and controlled personality.

According to the model, all of us occasionally get involved in each of the seven team role behaviour patterns. Mostly however we tend to use and be effective in only two or three of these behaviour patterns, as a result of our personality. Consequently for a group to achieve high levels of task performance it needs to be composed of individuals whose collective behaviour achieves a balance of all seven team behaviour patterns. It is as important that all seven are present as it is that there is no predominance of a particular one. For example, a group of five individuals, all of whom tend to behave in the 'co-ordinator' role, is likely to be perpetually dominated by a struggle for leadership. Equally a group of five which does not have anyone who is competent in the 'co-ordinator' role will be characterised by an absence of leadership and direction. The key requirement according to this approach is that a balance of all seven behaviour patterns must be present in a group. The precise balance is dictated by the nature of the problem being tackled by the group.

Because most people can perform two or three of the team behaviour patterns effectively, this approach can be applied to groups of less than seven people. Experience suggests that it can be effectively applied in groups of between four and twelve people. As groups with over twelve members tend to operate in a different way, the value of this approach to larger groups tends to be limited.

Application of the Team Role Model involves an assessment of individual group members' capacities to fulfil the seven team behaviour patterns. While this can be undertaken by a questionnaire, it can be better achieved through direct observation of behaviour. Application of the model to already established groups within an organisation uses the Behaviour Technology principles of examining actual group behaviour, and then encouraging the group to make decisions to change as a result of their own evaluation of their behaviour and performance. I used this approach[8] to assist a senior management team in charge of a business to improve their effectiveness. During a two-day workshop, the managers assessed their own behaviour from a closed circuit television recording of their discussion of a work problem. Because the seven team roles were only explained to the group after the recording was made, the Model itself could not have influenced the discussion. From the review of the recording, it became apparent to the group that it contained two 'critics', and that the roles of 'co-ordinator' and 'inspector' were not being adequately fulfilled. The remainder of the workshop was devoted to assisting the managers to develop further awareness of each other, and to draw up behaviour action plans which would achieve a better balance of the Team Roles and thereby improve the performance of the group. As a result of the workshop, the senior management team felt they worked more effectively together and were better able to manage the business for which they were responsible.

The significance of the Team Role Model is that is application embodies the fundamental ideas of Behaviour Technology. Application involves developing managers' awareness of their own behaviour with colleagues, using a framework which includes both problem-solving and emotional behaviours. Each of the team roles refers to specific observable behaviour, which can be assessed in the real world. Of particular importance is the fact that the Team Role Model is not just a conceptual tool but one which has importance for the achievement of task objectives. Finally, the model acknowledges the capacity we have for change, and provides us with a practical vehicle for bringing about behavioural change for the achievement of business outcomes.

Despite the encouraging results so far achieved with the Team Role Model, its validity has not yet been sufficiently demonstrated to become universally applicable. Nevertheless the model has value in assisting managers to adopt those behaviours which are required in their own groups so that business results can be more effectively achieved.

AN EXAMPLE OF A BEHAVIOUR TECHNOLOGY ANALYSIS OF A GROUP DISCUSSION

An example of how a group discussion can be analysed using the Problem-Solving Dimensions and Transactional Analysis is given below. The discussion involves a group of personnel managers representing particular sites in a division of a large corporation, together with the division personnel manager:

Division personnel manager: Corporate, as you know, have agreed that we can pay a disturbance allowance when employees relocate between sites over a short distance away from one another. While I feel that this is the right thing to do, I want to delay payment in our division until the issue of backdating is resolved. Our aim, as you know, is to backdate all payments for staff who relocated since last October, otherwise people who have already changed offices will complain that they were unfairly deprived of the allowance. Are you all clear therefore that we will not pay the allowance until the issue of backdating is sorted out?

Robin: That's all very well, but other divisions have been paying disturbance payments since December. I want to help our employees and treat them fairly, so let's just pay it now. I'm fed up with waiting until those bureaucrats in Corporate make up their mind. Let's pay it now.

Peter: Which division paid the allowance and for which move?

Robin: Manufacturing paid it in December up in Manchester when twenty-five people moved eight miles as a result of the closure of the stores. If they got the money, then it's only fair that our people also get it now for moves last autumn.

Division personnel manager: That's out of the question. You can't go independent. John is discussing the matter with Corporate on our behalf and will advise you when a decision is made so that you can implement it.

Alan: What about the question of distance moved? Many people in London who relocate three miles are as much affected as anyone out in the sticks moving ten miles. You don't get around London like driving down a country lane, you know. Two miles can mean a lot of extra hassle for people, an extra underground journey, another bus change or an extra twenty minutes in a traffic jam. I suggest we change the rule in London to any relocation of offices which is more than walking distance — say, half a mile.

Division personnel manager: No way. The rule says five miles and I am not going to change it.

Mary: I'm not clear why we have the five miles limit. After all, any change of location can involve potential redundancy and therefore, on that basis, some disturbance is involved if the individual is inconvenienced. Surely we should be paying the allowance to anyone who has to travel further to work as a result of a company change of location?

Division personnel manager: That's enough. I want to move on to the next item — we are behind time. No one can pay the allowance now and John will advise you of the Corporate ruling. If that gives anyone particular problems, discuss them with John.

This discussion contains a number of different types of behaviour. Before reading further, analyse what happened in terms of which Problem-Solving Dimensions and which ego states were used.

In his opening speech, the division personnel manager explains the Corporate ruling on the disturbance allowance, which is problem analysis. He goes on to express his support for this, 'While I feel that this is the right thing to do,' which is Adult. He then goes on to explain his reasoning for deferring payment until the backdating question is resolved, which is Parent and involves judgement. He finishes with 'Are you all clear. . . ', which is an example of leadership and Critical Parent.

Robin then counters with additional information about what other divisions do, which is problem analysis, and then goes into Nurturing Parent when he says 'I want to help our employees', followed by Critical Parent in his comments about Corporate. Peter responds with an Adult question which involves problem analysis. Robin answers with his Adult, with problem analysis data about which and when employees have received disturbance payments. He then returns to Nurturing Parent with 'If they got the money, then it's only fair that our people also get it now'.

The division personnel manager cuts the conversation short with a Critical Parent comment, 'That's out of the question.' He then uses his

Adult for planning and organising, 'John is discussing the matter with Corporate on our behalf and will advise you when a decision is made so that you can implement it.'

Alan then introduces a new theme with problem analysis and initiative concerning the issue of distance relocated. His argument also involves persuasiveness when he suggests changing the rules, judgement and an element of leadership. The division personnel manager responds negatively to this with Critical Parent. Mary takes up the wider issue raised by Alan previously and uses problem analysis and judgement. The division personnel manager decides to cut short the discussion with Critical Parent and Leadership. His final comment, 'If that gives anyone particular problems, discuss them with John,' involves delegation.

This same discussion can also be considered in terms of the games being played here. Because our analysis only involves a script, we cannot consider the non-verbal behaviour going on in the group. Despite the considerable amount of rational talk, apparently about the problem in hand, there may well be a game here between the group and the division personnel manager. In essence, the discussion involves the division personnel manager making a ruling and then a series of objections being raised by the other group members. Each of these objections is greeted by a Critical Parent decision by him. If this cycle of discussion is repeated at this group's regular meetings, it sounds as if the division personnel manager is playing Now I've Got You, You Son of a Bitch, which involves him in putting everyone down while appearing to allow an open interchange. In return, the group members are doing their utmost to play Blemish with the decisions of the division personnel manager. The covert message from the group members to the division personnel manager is that there is something wrong with his decisions.

The importance of game analysis is that it can potentially uncover the real issues affecting the group, which underlie the apparently logical and rational discussion going on. The acid test of whether games are being played depends on assessment of the non-verbal communication in the group.

Behaviour Technology can provide useful insights into the working of groups. While much of the previous research on groups has tended to be descriptive, neat conceptual models, including the Team Role Model, do not provide the answers. Rather, it is suggested here that we need frameworks which will help us understand the facts of behaviour in a group. Armed with the TA ego states and game theory as well as the Problem-Solving Dimensions, we can obtain a thorough understanding of what is going on in a group. If we find that achievement of the group's task objectives is not as effective as might be desired, the road to improved performance relies on increased understanding by group members of the obstacles and barriers which hold their performance back. With this understanding, the group can then draw up action plans on how to change their behaviour so that desired objectives can be achieved.

REFERENCES

1) Krech, D. and Crutchfield, R.S., *Theory and Problems of Social Psychology*, McGraw Hill, 1948.
2) Rothlisberger, F.J. and Dickson, W.J., *Management and the Worker*, Harvard Press, 1939.
3) Bales, R.F. and Slater, P.E., 'Role Differentiation in Small Decision Making Groups', in T. Parsons and R.F. Bales (eds), *Family, Socialisation and Interaction Processes*, Free Press, 1955.
4) Rackham, N., Honey, P. and Colbert, M., *Developing Interactive Skills*, Wellens Publishing, 1971.
5) Trist, E.L. and Bamforth, K.W., 'Selections from Social and Psycological Consequences of the Longwall Method of Coal Getting', *Human Relations*, 1951, 4,1.
6) Rice, A.K., *Productivity and Social Organisation in the Ahmedabad Experiment*, Tavistock, 1958.
7) Belbin, M., *Management Teams − Why they Succeed or Fail*, Heinemann, 1981.
8) Wellin, M., 'How to Manage by Groups', *Management Today*, February, 1978.

8 Managing people

Managing or leading people involves exercising control over others in order
to achieve results. Even if we do not have formal responsibility for others
or the title of manager, we all have scope in our jobs for managing people.
Personnel officers, systems analysts and marketing consultants all partly
rely for their success on their ability to exercise a degree of management
or leadership over those they work with, even if their formal authority for
doing so is nil. Traditionally, the role of managing people is one that rests
solely with line managers. Nevertheless, the organisation of today, and
even more the organisation of tomorrow, relies on staff specialists in
finance, personnel, information processing and other areas to influence
line management to ensure the effective achievement of organisation
objectives. The techniques of 'Matrix Management' or 'Duel Line
Reporting' bear this out.

In the same way that all jobs in an organisation allow some scope for
management of others, all jobs also involve acting as subordinate to
someone else. Even the chief executive of a large company, while charged
with direct responsibility for all people and resources within the
organisation, will be subordinate to others, e.g. the board of directors, the
shareholders, and government officials. Managing people is therefore
something we are all involved in, both as initiators of influence over others
and as receivers of others' influence over us.

Definitions of leadership abound, but for our purposes I propose to
adopt a simple definition of leadership as influence over others to achieve
an objective. Thus the leader of a department is the individual who
exercises most influence over others towards the achievement of department objectives. In most organisations, the function of leadership is shared
to a degree between members of a department, as was suggested in the
previous chapter, even though there may be one individual who exercises
more leadership than others. This may or may not be the same individual
who is formally designated as leader. However, as Behaviour Technology
is concerned with what people actually do, our main interest will be the
individual who exercises greatest leadership in a particular situation rather
than the one who is merely designated leader.

This chapter reviews recent thinking on managing people in the context
of Behaviour Technology. As with group working, most of the recent
approaches are concerned with what managers actually do, and can there-

fore be directly translated into the terms of Behaviour Technology. The final part of the chapter gives a number of leadership situations which you, the reader, are invited to evaluate from the point of view of current leadership thinking as well as from a Behaviour Technology perspective.

THE 'GREAT MAN' APPROACH TO LEADERSHIP

This view of leadership regards the possession of particular qualities as the main reason why certain individuals are able to guide, direct and lead others. It is particularly popular among historians and philosophers, and has frequently been used as justification to support the existence of élites within society — not only Hitler's view of the German people as the master race but also the British public school system! Although popular in the early development of psychology, the Great Man approach to leadership has since become less influential for a number of reasons.

Detailed reviews of research give some evidence which suggests that leaders tend to be more intelligent, extrovert, self-assured and concerned with achievement than others.[1] There are, however, too many ommissions from and exceptions to this view of leadership to justify it as a tenable approach on its own. Specifically, this view takes no account of the situation in which the leader operates. From our own experience we may know that the requirements for effective leadership in the armed forces are different from those in a small family firm. While personal characteristics may be one factor which influences leadership performance, it can be concluded that the demands of the situation faced by a leader are also significant in determining the qualities required. The possession of a 'charismatic personality' is not in itself sufficient to make someone a leader.

Related to this is the problem of how to develop leadership. In today's results-orientated world the concern of many business organisations is the development of employees to fulfil leadership roles. Viewing leadership as merely the possession of inherent traits implies that leaders are born and cannot be developed. Many organisations have discovered to their cost that possession of certain characteristics alone will not necessarily mean that the employee will become an effective leader.

From a practical point of view the Great Man approach leaves many questions unanswered, such as how leadership skills can be developed and which attributes are most important for a leader in a particular situation. This approach also tells us nothing about what leaders actually *do* differently from followers.

THE STYLE APPROACH TO LEADERSHIP

When it was realised that the Great Man approach to leadership did not provide useful answers, investigators adopted an alternative strategy. Instead of examining the inherent attributes of leaders, attention was given to the 'style' or manner of leaders' behaviour towards their subordinates. One of the best known exponents of this view is Douglas McGregor, who coined the phrases 'Theory X' and 'Theory Y'. McGregor's basic premise was that managers who created conditions which encouraged subordinates to achieve organisational goals through the achievement of their own personal goals (Theory Y), were more effective than those who merely coerced, directed or threatened subordinates to achieve results (Theory X).[2]

The significance of this approach is that it concentrates on what leaders do rather than what they are. By examining the behaviour of the leader it is possible to view leadership as an activity. This also implies that leadership is an interaction between the leader and those being led and is not merely dependent on the leader himself in isolation.

From the point of view of Behaviour Technology, the two-dimension approach to leadership is highly significant. As well as drawing attention to the fact that leadership is essentially about behaviour this approach emphasises that leadership is concerned with people as well as with achieving end results. In other words, leadership involves expressing feelings as well as problem-solving behaviours. Concern with people alone or with task alone is insufficient to result in effective leadership.

The two-dimension approach to leadership emerged in the 1950s and still largely dominates managers' thinking today. Various experts have further subdivided the two basic dimensions of 'concern for people' and 'concern for task', but even using these more detailed subdivisions of leadership style does not resolve the question of what it is that makes an effective leader. Instead, a more detailed categorisation of leadership behaviours, as opposed to styles, is required. Whether our concern is selecting managers, improving the performance of existing managers, or developing junior employees to become managers in the future, we need a more precise framework than four or six management styles to make it possible to understand and describe what a leader does, and then assess and develop individuals against these behavioural criteria. The Behaviour Technology framework of Transactional Analysis and the Problem-Solving Dimensions provides such a vehicle.

THE SITUATION APPROACH TO LEADERSHIP

To be effective a manager needs more than a framework for evaluating his or her own leadership behaviour. As important as their own behaviour are the demands placed on them by the situation in which they operate. The leadership requirements of an army officer on the battlefield are radically different from those of the research and development manager in a laboratory. In the former situation the leader will need to be quick and decisive, while in the latter these behaviours will be much less important than a style which harnesses the department's creative talents towards the solution of the organisation's product development goals; the research and development manager needs to be more creative than the army officer, and to use more complex problem analysis and greater sensitivity to subordinates. The two leadership situations place radically different demands on the leader and so not surprisingly will require different leadership behaviours.

In the 1960s, Fred Fiedler developed the Contingency Model of Leadership[3] which proposed that the style adopted by a leader should depend on the favourableness of the leadership situation. After conducting investigations in a number of organisations, he concluded that both in situations with high and very low leadership favourableness, group effectiveness was enhanced by a more autocratic leadership style, while more democratic styles were found to be most effective in situations of moderate leadership favourableness. While the army officer on the battlefield would be in an extremely unfavourable leadership situation, the research and development manager would tend to operate in situations of moderate leadership favourableness.

The importance of Fiedler's and others' work on the impact of leadership situations is that they reflect a long recognised reality, namely that a leader needs to take account of the situation in which he is operating when deciding which style to adopt.

Interesting as such models are, they leave some difficult questions unanswered for the practising manager. Even assuming that they are correct, the problem of how to assess the precise leadership situation in which a manager finds himself needs to be considered. The methods available are at best imprecise and difficult to use. Even the neat decision tree produced by Vroom for determining the appropriate leadership style to be used[4] covers only some of the many factors which could be taken into account. The outstanding requirement, therefore, is for a method which enables a manager (as opposed to a research psychologist), to assess the leadership situation in which he finds himself.

Evaluating leadership situations is made more complex when national and organisational values are brought into the picture. Americans have a different outlook on authority from the British, who in turn have a different outlook from the Japanese. Even within one nation, different companies have different ideas about what is expected from a leader in terms of management style. In some organisations, leadership is implemented through the formal regulations each department has for its work, as occurs in most bureaucracies. Other organisations are dominated by a central individual or group from whom all key decisions emanate rather than being run according to any procedures or regulations. This type of style often characterises small and medium sized companies. Clearly, the requirements for effective leadership in these two very different types of organisation will vary enormously. While obeying the formal rules may be a prerequisite for leadership in bureaucracies, it is unlikely to be of much significance in an organisation dominated by a powerful controlling individual or group.

THE BEHAVIOUR TECHNOLOGY APPROACH TO LEADERSHIP

There are no simple answers to the problem of leadership effectiveness. Rather it depends on the interaction of many complex factors, including the task and relationships within the group to be led, the culture within which it operates and the behaviour of the leader himself or herself. The very complexity of the issues involved suggest that it is unlikely, in the short term, that leadership can be reduced to general principles or theories. Instead of incomplete theory, a more fruitful approach might be to provide the manager with a framework with which they can carry out a diagnosis of the situation with a view to selecting a leadership style. At first glance this might seem an unreasonable burden to place on the manager's shoulders. Nevertheless, if the manager is able to use the framework for most management problem situations, the investment in learning and developing competence in its use may be more than worthwhile.

The framework of Transactional Analysis and the Problem-Solving Dimensions has already been used to assess the performance requirements of a job in Chapter 4 and group working in Chapter 7. The next step is to use this framework for evaluating leadership behaviour.

The 'concern for people' aspects of leadership are reflected in the Transactional Analysis concepts of stroking (giving recognition), use of the Nurturing Parent and Child ego states, parallel transactions and avoidance of games. These specific behaviours will all assist the development and maintenance of constructive relationships with others.

The 'concern for task' aspects of leadership can be defined in terms of the Problem-Solving Dimensions. Those of particular relevance are delegation, planning, decisiveness, initiative, flexibility/adaptability, risk taking, tenacity, sensitivity, persuasiveness, management control, problem analysis and judgement. The behaviours specified by the dimension of leadership itself are also relevant. The Critical Parent ego state from TA is also likely to be a part of the leader's behavioural repertoire to emphasise 'concern for task'.

Together, TA and the Problem-Solving Dimensions provide a means for categorising precise leader behaviours which encompass both concern for people and concern for task. While other behaviour frameworks such as Bales' Interaction Matrix (considered in Chapter 7) or Rackham and Honey's Behaviour Analysis[5] could also be used for this purpose, neither provides such detailed understanding.

As well as developing an understanding of leader behaviour, TA and the PSDs can be used by leaders to evaluate the leadership requirements of their work environments. A leader can use TA to understand the behaviour of his subordinates and plan appropriate responses which will assist achievement of performance objectives. If, for example, a subordinate predominantly uses their Nurturing Parent ego state, the manager might predict that use of his or her own Adapted Child would encourage the subordinate to achieve results through providing an opportunity to express their Nurting Parent. Alternatively, if the subordinate used extensive Free Child, the boss might want either to develop the working relationship by using his own Free Child or alternatively to curb the subordinate's Free Child by use of his Critical or Nurturing Parent.

Depending on the task, the manager can decide whether he or his subordinate should be undertaking problem analysis, judgement, and so on. Will the nature of the task require detailed management control or can this occur less frequently? Will initiative need to be taken to solve the problem or will it be resolved by existing routinised activities? Using the Problem-Solving Dimensions, the manager can assess the requirements of the situation in which he or she is working so that appropriate emphasis can be given to the dimensions which best assist the achievement of objectives.

Two examples will be given of leader behaviour with subordinates. After analysing the behaviour of the leader draw your own conclusions about how effective you believe this was, and consider alternative behaviours which the leader might have used.

EXAMPLE ONE

Boss: I'd like you to produce a paper for sales managers predicting the rate at which salesmen are likely to leave the company next year. The sort of thing I have in mind is a two or three page report, with an analysis of the reasons salesmen tend to leave, and a best estimate of how many losses we can expect next year. Can you have it ready by the end of next week?

Subordinate: Yes, but we've talked about the problem of salesmen leaving and there are so many possible reasons that it is impossible to be absolutely accurate.

Boss: You're right, it is a complex subject, but I believe we need to give sales managers a best estimate of what to expect next year and I would like you to produce this.

Subordinate: It's so very difficult to forecast ahead because we can't be sure of what state the economy will be in and that has a critical impact on turnover.

Boss: It's not that difficult because you can go to our Corporate Planning Department and ask for their projection for the economy next year and use that in your work. You've already met the manager of the department and I'm sure he will help you.

Subordinate: None of the statistical methods we have are any good, so there is no point in producing a paper when all the sales managers need to do is look at the current quarterly figures on turnover and that will tell them all they need to know.

Boss: They can look at the latest manpower figures but very few of them ever do — that's the whole point. I want you to bring the problem of salesman turnover to their attention, so that they will realise how much effort we have to put into replacing salesmen who leave.

Subordinate: The only thing that will make the sales managers think about the problem is if we identify the costs of recruiting replacements, but our system does not allow us to obtain accurate costings, so there is no point in producing a report which doesn't contain costs.

On one level, the discussion is about the difficulties faced by a subordinate in completing a report about salesman turnover. In his first statement, the boss used leadership: 'I'd like you to produce . . .', 'The sort of thing I have in mind is . . .'. The boss then attempts management control with the statement: 'Can you have it ready by the end of next week?'. The subordinate responds with a series of detailed points about why the task should not be tackled. On the surface, these seem to involve problem analysis: 'the problem of salesmen leaving' and 'there are so many possible reasons', followed by a series of judgements: 'It's so very difficult to forecast ahead because . . .', 'None of the statistical methods we have are any good,' 'The only thing that will make the sales managers think about the problem is if we identify the costs of recruiting replacements,' and later 'our system does not allow us to obtain accurate costings, so there is no point in producing a report which doesn't contain costs.'

The boss attempts to counter these negative judgements with problem analysis, e.g. 'you can go to our Corporate Planning Department and ask them for their projection for the economy'. Then he uses more direction and delegation with: 'I want you to bring the problem of salesman turn-over to their attention'.

On the surface, this conversation may seem rational. Closer examination of the dialogue, however, suggests that something else is going on between the boss and subordinate. How would you react at this stage if you were the boss? Would you continue to argue with the subordinate's apparent objections? Before reading further, decide what you would say to the subordinate and why.

What appears to be going on here is not so much a rational and logical conversation but an exchange between boss and subordinate which involves the latter in arguing against the suggestions and ideas of the former. Every time the boss counters the subordinate's point, the subordinate raises another objection as to why he should not write the report. If we view this conversation from the point of view of the feelings expressed between the participants, we gain an alternative picture of what is going on here. The manager starts with an apparently Adult request 'I'd like you to produce a paper for sales managers', and then continues in the same vein. The subordinate responds with a series of apparently Adult objections: 'it's impossible to be absolutely accurate', 'it's so very difficult to forecast ahead', 'none of the statistical methods we have are any good'. Nevertheless, these are not so much judgements based on data but more like a series of ulterior Critical Parent comments intended to divert the boss from the intended piece of work. While we do not have a record of the subordinate's non-verbal behaviour to substantiate this point, the number of negative reasons raised for not producing the report suggest that they are not based on logic but rather that a game of Yes But is going on. Every time the boss raises an issue or counters a previous point, the subordinate raises another. Each suggestion raised by the boss is greeted by a Critical Parent response from the subordinate.

What has occurred is clearly not a constructive interchange between boss and subordinate likely to lead to a positive solution of the task in hand. The boss will have to rethink his approach to get the subordinate to tackle the problem of salesman turnover. Using the Behaviour Technology framework, the boss can analyse the preferred behaviours used by the subordinate and then adapt his style so that a more positive response is achieved.

The behaviours used by the subordinate in the above example suggest high levels of problem-solving skills, particularly problem analysis, planning and organising and judgement. We also know that the subordinate has a well developed Critical Parent as shown by the Yes But game. Thus the most effective course open to the boss is likely to be one of harnessing the subordinate's problem-solving skills by manipulating his Critical Parent ego state, so that these skills can be directed towards solving the salesman turnover problem. One way of achieving this might be for the boss to use Critical Parent behaviour towards the sales management over the salesman turnover problem, thus encouraging the subordinate to use his skills to tackle the issue. The conversation might then go as follows:

EXAMPLE TWO

Boss: Our company just doesn't seem able to keep salesmen. Sales managers must be doing the wrong things and their incompetence is costing the company a lot of wasted resources. What do you think we can do to make sales managers aware of the problem of salesmen leaving?

Subordinate: There are so many reasons salesmen leave the company. Some of them must be leaving because of poor treatment by sales managers.

Boss: That's right, and I think we need to show our sales managers what they are doing wrong so that they can be aware of the need to change their methods of management. How can we do that?

Subordinate: I think we should find out the facts about why salesmen leave and then present them to senior management. They'll then know who is to blame for the problem.

Boss: How would you do that?

Subordinate: Well, I could analyse the leaving reports of the salesmen who have left the company and put a complete picture together. I might produce a report and also do a presentation at one of the staff meetings — that would let them know who's to blame.

Boss: I like that idea. One of the objections the sales managers will come up with is that the problem only applies to this time of year, and that in a few months, when we are out of the main recruiting season, there'll be no problem. I don't want to let them wriggle out of their responsibilities. How could we show them that there will continue to be a problem next year unless they take some action now?

Subordinate: Well, I know how to get them on that one. We could project the leaving trends forward so that this would show how many salesmen will leave next year.

Boss: That's good. We have an opportunity to present the case at the management meeting at the end of next week when the sales managers will be discussing the results for the first quarter. Could you have a paper ready for that meeting with a presentation that would really show them?

Subordinate: I'll do that. That would put them under the spotlight.

In this example, the boss's behaviour differs considerably from that in the first example. The important change is in his use of Critical Parent towards sales management as demonstrated by: 'Sales managers must be doing the wrong things', 'we need to show our sales managers what they are doing wrong', 'I don't want to let them wriggle out of their responsibilities,' and finally, 'that would really show them', instead of directing pressure towards the subordinate.

So instead of telling the subordinate what to do and creating resistance, the boss is encouraging him by directing his Critical Parent against sales management. The boss is also encouraging the subordinate's problem-solving skills within his Adult by using phrases such as: 'What do you think we can do to make sales managers aware of the problem of salesmen leaving?' 'How can we do that?' 'How could we show them that there will continue to be a problem next year unless . . .'. The subordinate responds with considerable problem-solving behaviour, e.g. 'There are so many reasons salesmen leave' (judgement), 'I think we should find out the facts about why salesmen leave and then present them to senior management' (planning and organising), and later, 'Well, I know how to get them on that one. We can project the leaving trends forward' (judgement and problem analysis).

At the game level of analysis, there are some interesting things going on here. The boss has set up a game of Ain't It Awful and, potentially, Now I've Got You, You Son of a Bitch against sales management. The inter-change of transactions has got the subordinate committed to writing the report; however, he is also spoiling to set up NIGYYSOB with sales managers and this could create future problems. Despite this, the boss's immediate problem with the subordinate has been resolved.

Behaviour Technology provides an alternative strategy for looking at issues of leadership in place of the traditional methods available. Instead of prescriptive frameworks, Behaviour Technology provides a platform for the practising manager to understand the behaviour of subordinates and the task behaviours required. With this data base the manager can consider alternative strategies and options for maximising leadership behaviour, so that the desired follower/subordinate behaviour is facilitated. Behaviour Technology recognises that organisational behaviour is not a precisely measurable phenomenon with clear-cut inputs and outputs. The effective manager will rather need to understand behaviour in its full complexity, so that he can plan and implement alternative leadership strategies until the desired results are achieved.

REFERENCES

1) Mann, R.D., 'A Review of the Relationship between Personality and Performance in Small Groups', *Psychological Bulletin*, 1959, 56.
2) McGregor, D.M., *The Human Side of Enterprise*, McGraw Hill, 1960.
3) Fiedler, F., 'Validation and Extension of the Contingency Model of Leadership Effectiveness', *Psychological Bulletin*, 1971, 76, 128—48.
4) Vroom, V.H. and Yetton, P.W., *Leadership and Decision Making*, University of Pittsburg Press, 1973.
5) Rackham, N., Honey, P. and Colbert, M., *Developing Interactive Skills*, Wellens Publishing, 1971.

9　Assessment centres

Because business organisations are not behavioural science laboratories where new methods and techniques can be readily adopted, you may well have reservations about the practicality of adopting Behaviour Technology. Day to day business problems need to be resolved before the adoption of new methods and techniques can be considered. This chapter is concerned with assessment centres, the major area in which Behaviour Technology has become an established method of human resource problem-solving. The number of organisations using assessment centres in Europe is growing fast and includes respected names such as the Ford Motor Company, Mars, Xerox, IBM, ICL and the British armed forces and civil service. In the United States, assessment centres are already widely used as a method of employee selection and development.

After defining what is an assessment centre and the way it differs from traditional assessment devices, a number of wider issues involved in their use will be considered. These include the structure of assessment centre events and the method by which assessment occurs as well as questions concerning assessors, candidates and wider organisation issues.

WHAT IS AN ASSESSMENT CENTRE?

Assessment centres can serve a variety of purposes and may take many different forms. Whatever their specific purpose, their primary output is an evaluation of individual skills based on actual performance in tackling problems. This assessment is mostly used either for selection purposes or for training and development.

The significance of this process is that the evaluation is based on the observed behaviour of the candidate. Traditional methods of assessment, in particular the interview, rely on indirect reports of behaviour, as given by the candidate in response to questions posed by the interviewer. Selection tests also rely on indirect assessment of candidates' job behaviour, based on the way they respond to questions posed, mostly of a paper and pencil type.

Another unique feature of assessment centres is that they involve assessment on tasks or activities which simulate those of the job or job type against which the candidate is being evaluated. Although interviewers may elicit details of how a candidate tackled a particular problem in the past, this will mostly relate to a different context than the one for which assessment is being made. If a supervisor is being assessed for promotion into management, an interview may identify how he handled past situations or behaved when tackling certain types of problems in his current job, but the interview can provide little information on how he would react to similar problems if he were fulfilling a management role. To assume that the problem is the same whether faced by a supervisor or a manager may well not be valid. The personal relations of supervisors with their subordinates may be closer than those a manager has with his subordinates. Therefore while a supervisor may deal with a particular problem in one way with his subordinates, this may not help to predict the behaviour of that same supervisor if he were to be promoted to a management position.

Assessment centres ensure the relevance of candidate behaviour by enabling evaluation to take place in structure task situations which resemble the job or job type against which assessment takes place. If we want to assess whether an operator has the skills necessary to make an effective supervisor, the assessment centre would contain tasks which closely resembled those found in a supervisor's job, both in terms of content and context. If we wished to assess at an interview how an operator would handle a subordinate whose performance was below the standard required, we could ask the operator to give a theoretical answer to this hypothetical problem. The candidate's response would be governed by the theoretical knowledge he had of such situations. In many factory environments, for example, it is possible to identify operatives who perform below standard by data from machine output, time clocks, and so on; but in real life an operator would never have used hard data to solve such problems. An assessment centre might assess an individual's ability at dealing with poor subordinate performance by placing him in a structured problem situation involving the same kind of poor performance as he would find in a supervisory job for which he was being selected. Such a problem situation might involve a role playing exercise, an 'in-tray' or a fact finding exercise, all of which can be structured in a way which closely resemble the situation found on the job.

As assessment centres involve direct assessment of candidates' behaviour in tackling problems which resemble those found in the job against which the candidate is being assessed, this raises important issues. These include the process by which observation and assessment is made, by whom, the method of simulating the job against which assessment occurs, and the purpose for which the assessment is made. These and other questions are addressed in the following sections.

ASSESSMENT CRITERIA

Setting up an assessment centre requires decisions about the dimensions or criteria against which candidates are to be assessed. Because assessment centres focus on the actual behaviour and performance of candidates, the criteria used will be behavioural and could evaluate either problem-solving behaviour or expression of feelings, or both. This contrasts with the criteria used at many selection interviews which are mostly non-behavioural and instead focus on overall experience or biographical data. Typically interviews dwell on details of examinations passed and the work experience of the candidate. Thus an interview for selection of a personnel officer might prove the extent to which candidates had experience of interviews, conducting training courses and writing job descriptions. In contrast to this, an assessment centre for selection of a personnel officer would use behavioural criteria which contributed to success in these activities. Some of the behaviours which contribute to conducting interviews and training courses include listening skills, planning and organising, interpersonal sensitivity, persuasieveness and oral communication. Ability to move between all the TA ego states, especially the Adult, Nurturing Parent and Adapted Child, would also be important.

At first sight, it may seem that assessment of individual behaviour and experience amount to the same thing. The two are however fundamentally different. If we establish that a candidate has had experience of running training courses this may not enable us to decide whether they were effective or ineffective at this activity, but merely that they had run training courses. However, if the candidate had no experience of this activity, it becomes particularly difficult to assess whether they could be effective at it in the future. On the other hand, if we actually observed and evaluated their skills of listening, planning, oral communication and persuasiveness, we could decide whether they had the potential to run training courses effectively. We could then assess the likelihood of whether the candidate could make an effective trainer, whether or not they had ever run a training course. This contrasts with the simple experience criteria which would not enable an assessment to be made of candidates who had no previous experience of running training courses.

Whereas interview assessment criteria may include different types — biographic, experience, attainment — assessment centres criteria need to be behavioural in nature, i.e. observable. The behavioural criteria used need to be rigorously defined and understood by the assessor in order that an assessment can be made. While this might appear also to be the case with interview criteria, much evidence suggests that it is not. Interviewers frequently make an assessment of the candidate based on whether they like the individual or find him socially acceptable, and though the final assessment may suggest that the candidate has the required experience and background for the job, nevertheless, this will frequently be based on subjective factors.

Utilising behavioural criteria to assess individuals' suitability for a job or to identify development and training needs requires an evaluation of the behaviour and performance requirements for that job. In the example quoted above, it is likely that listening, oral communications, planning and persuasiveness would be required for running training centres. Nevertheless the precise order of importance of these or other behavioural criteria will depend on the nature of the training course. Interpersonal skills training requires different skills from those required to teach advanced mathematics. Once the behaviours for running training courses have been determined, it is still necessary to identify situations in the job which are important for successful performance.

Identification of assessment criteria is a prerequisite for setting up an assessment centre and will influence the way it is designed. Chapter 4 described the methods by which job performance and behaviour requirements can be identified and these methods are largely used by assessment centre designers in selecting assessment criteria. There is considerable evidence that problem-solving behaviours and expression of feelings are equally important for success in many jobs. Returning to our earlier example of a personnel officer who is responsible for running training courses, we realise that however rational and logical the individual may be, they also need to take care of the trainees in their charge. Without expression of such feelings (i.e. Nurturing Parent) the trainer is unlikely to develop helpful relationships with trainees and this could prevent effective performance of the job.

JOB SIMULATIONS

Once the criteria for performance of a job have been identified, the assessment centre designer then needs to devise structured task situations which resemble those found in the job and which provide scope to use the required behaviours. All jobs of a managerial nature involve working in a number of situations, and these need to be identified with precision if we are to construct a simulation of the job. Whereas a personnel manager may spend part of his time conducting interviews with job applicants, he may also get involved in negotiating with trade union representatives and attending line management meetings as the personnel spokesman as well as managing subordinates in his own department. Most jobs operate in a number of different situations and you may want to reflect for a moment on the situations involved in your own job.

Job simulations clearly cannot be the actual job itself, otherwise the task of assessment would become unduly drawn out and resource consuming. Normally, simulations involved a series of structured problem situations in which candidates are directed to achieve a specific goal or objective. A typical job simulation exercise may be to ask questions about a problem with a view to identifying the root causes and to make a decision on how it should be solved. Another job simulation may require participation in a group discussing a problem, with the objective of arriving at a single solution which all group members support. Alternatively, the simulation could involve analysing quantitative business data and writing a report with proposals on improving the performance of the business.

Taken together the structured problem situations should represent the important work situations for the job against which assessment is to occur. Generally each problem situation may last between twenty minutes and three hours, depending on the nature of the task. There is no reason why an assessment centre exercise should last as long as the real work situations faced in the job. The intention rather is that the situations should allow the candidates being assessed to tackle the problem in a similar manner to that usually required on the job, even if the timescales are substantially reduced. For example, in an assessment centre designed to select a training consultant, it may be appropriate to have public speaking as one of the exercises. While lectures given by a training consultant may last an hour on the job, there is no reason why an assessment centre public speaking task should last for more than fifteen minutes. The behaviour elicited in a fifteen-minute public talk is likely to be representative of that same individual's behaviour in a one and a half hour talk. The public speaking criteria of oral communication, persuasiveness and planning can all be assessed within this timescale.

Assessment centre job simulation tasks can be devised for any of the situations which are to be found in a job. The extreme example of an assessment centre exercise is the use of flight simulators to recreate the cockpit environment for pilot training, as this is a 99 per cent replication of the job. Jobs may primarily involve working in groups, in one to one situations, or on one's own. Many assessment centres use group discussion as a task and these simulate situations where the job holder has to work with a group of others to solve a problem. The task could be one where each participant has different pieces of information which they need to share in order to solve a problem (as generally happens when managers from different functions meet). While the production manager might see the problem from a production cost perspective, the marketing man may perceive the same problem from the point of view of the customer, who is concerned with quality and reliability in relation to the offerings of the competition. In contrast to both, the personnel man may see a problem from the point of view of pay rates and union relationships. Group discussions may be used to simulate such real life situations. If a key part of the job against which assessment is being made involves leading a group, the group discussion would be designed so that leadership is open-ended, allowing individuals to bid for it. Alternatively, the group discussion problem may involve rotating the chairmanship of the group so that each group member is provided with an opportunity to display leadership skills.

Job simulations may also be devised for working with one other person such as a customer or subordinate. The most crucial job situation for many salesmen is the one to one discussion they have with customers. Therefore an assessment centre designed to select or develop salesmen may well contain a number of exercises where the candidate has to discuss a problem with a role player who is behaving like a typical customer. The role player might be instructed to be initially reluctant to make a commitment unless a particular problem they raise is dealt with by the candidate. Depending on how the participant reacts, the role player will respond. While job simulations involving role playing create demands on those fulfilling a role, in practice these can provide a very rich source of information on candidate behaviour. Whereas in a group discussion a candidate may only talk for a small proportion of the total time the group is working, in a one to one exercise with a role player the candidate would be expected to do most of the talking.

Many jobs involve working on one's own, either responding to memos and administrative queries or in writing reports. The former situations can be simulated by 'in-tray' exercises which require candidates to deal with a series of written items in a manager's in-tray. The items in the in-tray would usually be related to those found in the in-trays of jobs against which assessment occurs. Thus a sales manager's in-tray might contain salesmen's expense claims; a personnel manager's may contain details of a union claim, a disciplinary case, manpower planning data and papers of candidates who have applied for a job; and a financial manager's may contain financial reports, capital expenditure proposals, monthly accounts and directives for cost cutting from a director.

The briefing papers to the candidate would inform them of the company rules and requirements for handling these items and they would be assessed in part on the extent to which these had been applied in dealing with each item. The written responses of the candidate in the form of memos and the decisions made in handling each item provide extensive behavioural information with which candidates can be assessed against the criteria. In-tray exercises can be effective at assessing planning and organising, delegation, problem analysis, judgement, written communication and, to some extent, leadership and interpersonal sensitivity.

Devising assessment centre exercises is difficult and time consuming. While some organisations may develop their own, other companies purchase these ready made from consultants, for instance, DDI. In either case, it is critical that the contents of exercises are kept confidential and that candidates do not retain any papers after attending a centre.

ASSESSORS

The question of who should act as an assessor at an assessment centre remains the subject of considerable controversy. Should it be the personnel specialist, the line manager or someone else? This issue is particularly important in view of the very detailed information that is provided about candidates; far more than emerges from any other assessment method. It is also important in view of the extensive resources that are invested in designing and running an assessment centre, which are on an altogether different scale than an afternoon spent interviewing three or four job candidates.

Some organisations use as assessors the line managers who supervise individuals in the jobs against which assessment is being made. This has the advantage of bringing the knowledge and experience of managers to bear on the assessment process. It also has the important benefit of developing the commitment of managers to the final assessment. If a sales manager receives a detailed report on a job candidate he may react differently if he knows the assessment is the product of another experienced sales manager than if he knows it comes from someone in personnel who has no direct experience of a sales job. Another benefit of using line management as assessors is that they can provide direct feedback on the realism and relevance of the exercises to the job against which assessment is being made. If line managers find exercises unrealistic they will quickly comment on this, thereby encouraging the centre to be redesigned so that it simulates the job better. Line managers also bring their own views about the performance standards that they expect for job holders, which has the advantage of making assessment more job related. On the other hand this may be a disadvantage if managers' performance expectations are lower than they might be!

Other organisations prefer to place line managers or personnel specialists in assessor roles on a full-time basis for a period of time. This has the advantage of ensuring that there is always a body of assessors available, something which is not the case when line managers are requested to take a few days away from their jobs to take on the assessor role. Another advantage of this approach is that it makes it worthwhile to invest effort in the training of assessors as it is known they will be filling this role for a period of time.

While organisations may need to adopt different solutions to the question of who should act as assessors, the one fact that has been established with certainty is that assessors need to be trained to fulfil their role effectively. While many of us feel that we are skilled interviewers, evidence suggests that without special training we are generally very poor at observing and evaluating what people do. The contradictory evidence of court witnesses to the same incident under investigation bears this out.

Similarly with motor accidents — if a number of pedestrians observe the same accident, the reports of which car did what can vary markedly. So it is with untrained assessors at an assessment centre; without special training a group of assessors observing the same candidate tackling a job simulation will perceive different aspects of the candidate's behaviour, and consequently make widely different assessments about the candidate's skills.

Undergoing systematic assessor training may be seen as a waste of a manager's time. However most of us have never received any form of training in observing what people do or how they behave. We may have spent years learning to speak, read and write, but the amount of time we spent in learning to observe and listen objectively to others is minimal. Evidence suggests that without systematic training we draw conclusions about others based on subjective judgements. These may often be based on generalisations about people which we picked up in our childhood.

In everyday life we tend to draw conclusions about others at the same time as we are observing and interacting with them. While this may be necessary in many practical situations, it frequently leads us to confuse the facts of individual behaviour with the evaluations we draw from these facts. Consequently, after observing someone we may form an evaluation about the individual but not be able to recall the facts about what they actually did which resulted in that evaluation.

A simple example may perhaps bear this point out. If you see two young English men walking along holding hands, what would you assume about them? You might assume that they were gay. On the other hand, if you were in India and observed two young men walking hand in hand you would not be entitled to draw the same conclusion; in India, men commonly walk hand in hand as an indication of their friendship, without its denoting any sexual relationship. Inferring that someone is gay from one piece of information can lead to erroneous conclusions. Similarly we often draw conclusions about individuals' effectiveness at work from very limited data. In some companies a manager who is seen to leave work at the finishing time of 5.30 p.m. may be seen as disloyal because the norm for the company is that everyone who has the interests of the company at heart must work late. Once this evaluation has been made about a manager there is little he can do to change it, irrespective of how good the results he achieves may be.

You may regard these two examples of the way evaluations about people are formed as rather simplistic. Nevertheless, reflect for a moment on a manager you consider to be effective. What data do you have to support that evaluation?

No doubt you will be able to identify a number of specific instances of behaviour which support your evaluation of this effective manager. If you discussed these examples with a recruitment consultant, how impressed would he or she be that they genuinely indicated whether the individual was effective or not? Most of us are very confident about our ability to evaluate others but the information we use to support our assessment is, more often than not, less substantial than it might be. The merest suggestion that someone is not good at assessing others is as personal as the suggestion that someone is not a good driver or a good lover.

OBSERVING AND EVALUATING CANDIDATE PERFORMANCE

Evaluating candidate skills at an assessment centre differs from the way we evaluate others in everyday life. As well as placing more demands on the assessor, assessment centre evaluations are made against predetermined criteria or dimensions. In everyday life, we may make judgements about others because they feel right — he is a relaxed individual, she gets on easily with people — and these may or may not have a bearing on their ability to perform their job. We may be told that a particular individual has certain qualities like drive, aggressiveness or intelligence, but the extent to which these affect the individual's ability to achieve agreed results may not be questioned. Often when a manager speaks with awe about someone of high intelligence this is as much a reflection of the way the manager values intelligence as of whether the person's intelligence contributes to performance. Equally salesmen with drive may be held in esteem even if, when we enquire about the behavioural aspects of this much valued characteristic, we find that they cannot be defined.

Assessing candidate performance at an assessment centre involves four distinct stages: observation, recording, classifying and evaluation. The first two stages take place while the candidate is performing the designated tasks, or are taken from material produced as a direct result, for instance a video recording of the candidate. Before making any assessment the assessor will gather all the available data, most of which will consist of the things said by the candidate in a group discussion or a one to one exercise. To ensure that a full record of candidate behaviour is produced the assessor will record everything said and done by the candidate. This will include short interjections as well as complete sentences. Producing such a record is in itself demanding and requires complete concentration as well as quick writing; it should contain no judgements or interpretations.

In assessment centre tasks which involve writing a report or responding to an in-tray exercise, the process of recording has been performed by the candidate and therefore does not need to be undertaken by the assessor. The report or memo produced by the candidate is a record of his behaviour.

Once the record of candidate behaviour is available, the assessor can commence the task of classifying each item of behaviour against the criteria or dimensions to be used for the evaluation. If planning is a criterion, the assessor will review the record of candidate behaviour for instances where planning occurred, marking the script accordingly. Only when the complete record of behaviour has been classified on the relevant criteria can the process of evaluation take place. In any given exercise, particular parts will lend themselves to planning activities, e.g. drawing up a list of priority actions while tackling an in-tray, making appointments or cancelling appointments which clash, and drawing up an action plan to help a subordinate tackle a problem. Depending on the level of job and the nature of the assessment centre task, the candidate would be expected to demonstrate planning behaviour when tackling certain parts of a problem. The extent to which the candidate did or did not undertake planning activities as shown by the classification of his or her behaviour record would enable an evaluation to be made of this behavioural skill. If the candidate undertook effective planning behaviour at all appropriate points during an exercise, a high evaluation of this dimension would be given; alternatively, if very few or no instances of effective planning were noted in an exercise requiring planning, the candidate would be given a low evaluation. The assessment should be backed up by actual examples of what he or she actually did or did not do in response to a particular situation in the simulation exercise.

In practice, any particular piece of behaviour may constitute evidence on a number of different criteria or dimensions. If for example during an exercise a candidate said:

> I think what we need to do is leave this particular decision until we have analysed the financial data, because we don't have enough facts at our disposal at the moment. Can we return to it when we look at the balance sheet?

This sentence contains evidence on the criteria of judgement and planning. The candidate made a judgement that there is not sufficient data available to make a decision. Planning behaviour has taken place because the individual has put forward a proposal about when the decision should be made, namely, 'when we look at the balance sheet'.

The task facing the assessor with this piece of behaviour is to decide which criteria are best demonstrated. It is likely that planning and judgement are both important here. The final evaluation of this piece of information will however depend on the context in which it was said. If the group were reviewing how they should plan their activities then this statement has a different significance if the group had already spent considerable time in debating the particular decision in question. In the former case the judgement dimension would be more important, while in the latter the planning dimension would probably be more important.

Besides showing how any one piece of behaviour can act as evidence on more than one criterion, this example also shows the need to evaluate and classify behaviour within the context in which it takes place. The assessor will therefore need to have some record of what other behaviour is taking place as well as merely that being assessed. In one to one exercises as well as in group discussion, the assessor will find it useful to keep some general record of what is going on.

The processes of classifying and evaluating usually take at least as long as the process of observing and recording behaviour during the assessment centre exercise. Thus if a candidate was involved in a twenty-minute discussion the process of classifying behaviour can be expected to take twenty minutes, as can the process of evaluation.

After candidates have gone through all the assessment centre exercises the assessors meet to pool their data on individual candidates with a view to forming an overall evaluation of each. It is common that each candidate is observed by different assessors in each exercise on a centre, to minimise the possibility of evaluations being influenced by bias from any one assessor. If each candidate has been observed and assessed by five different assessors the likelihood of prejudice influencing the overall evaluation is reduced. Therefore when the assessors meet together each contributes equally to the final assessment made. A further factor which assists in arriving at an unbiased evaluation is having a chairman at the final evaluation who has not been involved in the assessment process; this may commonly be the assessment centre administrator whose role is to ensure the effective running of the centre.

ASSESSMENT CENTRES – FOR SELECTION OR DEVELOPMENT?

The output of an assessment centre will contain a detailed evaluation of each candidate's performance against the criteria assessed. Considerable controversy surrounds the exact purpose to which such an evaluation should be put. Some argue that in view of the detailed nature of the material gathered, assessment centres should primarily be used as a method of identifying individual development needs so that appropriate career and job development activities can be undertaken. Others suggest that the method can best be used as a means of making selection and placement decisions.

As with all such controversies, there are few absolute answers to how assessment centre output should be used. In practice the particular manpower priorities of the organisation running the centre will determine the use to which assessment centres are put. Nevertheless, some basic issues can be identified which organisations should take into account when deciding whether assessment centres are to be used primarily for selection or development.

When making selection decisions a manager will inevitably want to take account of a number of factors. While a major consideration will be whether a candidate has the necessary skills to perform the job, this is by no means the only criterion for selection. A manager is also likely to take into account whether the candidate is the sort of person he or she will want to work with, and whether the individual complements the other members of the department. Inevitably the former criterion will largely be subjective, while the latter will be difficult to evaluate in objective terms. So while an assessment centre can produce detailed information about a candidate's skills it will not yield information on whether the recruiting manager will like the candidate or not.

Other factors will also influence selection decisions over and above the possession of management skills, for instance technical knowledge and personal circumstances. These cannot usually be evaluated by observed behaviour at an assessment centre and will require alternative assessment methods including interviews. We can therefore conclude that an assessment centre can be used effectively as an input into selection decisions but not as the sole method of gathering information about candidates.

From the point of view of development, assessment centres have a number of unique benefits in comparison with other methods of evaluating individuals. While interviews can provide some development data, that derived from an assessment centre is far more detailed and diverse. Assessment centre evaluations also have the significant advantage of being backed up by hard behavioural data. If you were to tell me that I needed to develop my planning skills as a result of information gathered at an interview, you might have difficulty in providing evidence to support this assessment; but if you fed this conclusion back to me after my attendance at an assessment centre, you would almost certainly have extensive behavioural data available to back up your evaluation. If I challenged the basis of the recommendation you would be able to quote specific situations in which I had failed to plan as effectively as I might have done. This is one considerable advantage of assessment centres as a method for identifying employee development needs.

We can therefore conclude that assessment centres can serve both selection and development purposes. When used for selection the data from the centre should be considered as one input among others which contribute to the making of a selection decision. Irrespective of whether or not assessment centres are used primarily for development, the quality of the information produced has considerable value for development purposes, so it seems sensible to use it in this way even if the prime reason for running the centre is to select candidates for jobs.

The way in which assessment centre feedback data is provided to candidates will have a considerable effect on the candidate. It is considered good practice for one of the assessors to provide personal feedback to candidates, as this increases the likelihood that the candidate will accept the final verdict and also makes it easier to provide clear answers to any questions they might raise. Feedback data in the form of a written report alone suffers from being impersonal, and however well written will not cover all the areas about which the candidate may have questions.

HOW EFFECTIVE ARE ASSESSMENT CENTRES?

Undoubtedly the costs of running assessment centres — the resources required for setting up and managing them — are considerably greater than for other evaluation techniques. From my own experience it takes on average over two days of management time to make an assessment centre evaluation of one candidate; considerably more than for any interview assessment.

Assessment centres are not instant panacea for solving all human resource problems in business. What they do provide is the single most accurate method of evaluating individual management and behavioural skills. This conclusion is supported by a number of longitudinal follow-up studies carried out with assessment centre candidates on both sides of the Atlantic. The American Telephone and Telegraph Company was able to predict the likelihood of young entrants reaching middle management much more effectively with assessment centres than with conventional interviewing programmes.[1] In the British civil service a follow-up study over a twenty-year period also found that assessment centres were far more effective than alternative assessment devices for predicting future job success.

From my own involvement in running assessment centres for over a hundred candidates, the most frequently voiced criticism was that the centres sometimes provided a more negative evaluation of candidates than line management assessments. It was significant, however, that of all the promotion decisions made as a result of these assessments only one appears to have been considered inappropriate; a not unsatisfactory record by any yardstick.

Whether the added accuracy of evaluation provided by assessment centres is cost effective depends largely on the use made of the information. If assessment centre output is used as fully as possible as the basis for making accurate selection and development decisions for future middle and senior managers in an organisation, then it is likely to be amply cost justified; but if the technique is used as a gimmick or the results are not followed up by appropriate manpower actions in the areas of selection and development, or in reward systems, then the potential benefits of the process will be wasted. When they are used appropriately, however, an increasing number of highly profit-conscious organisations are finding that assessment centres can prove extremely valuable for making critical human resource decisions.

REFERENCE

1) Bray, D.W., Campbell, R.J. and Grant, D.L., *Formative Years in Business*, Robert E. Krieger, 1974.

10 Manpower development

Manpower development, including training programmes, succession plans, career structures, coaching and counselling, have the reputation of being soft options. While many managers acknowledge that these are intrinsically good things to do, they are seen to contribute at best indirectly to the achievement of organisation objectives. As a result development activities, while receiving lip service, are in practice given low priority, especially at a time of recession. Why is this the case and even more importantly is this in the best interests of the business?

If we talked to an accountant about eliminating or reducing the idle time of capital equipment we would almost certainly find him enthusiastic about the idea because of the reduction it would bring about in fixed costs per item of output. In a time of cost reductions, one of the first things to be reduced is spending on the improved utilisation of human resources. The different reaction to making better use of capital equipment, as opposed to making better use of human resources (which is what manpower development is aimed at), is curious and may well be attributable to the way these activities are viewed within a business.

Capital plant tends to be viewed as a financial asset with a specific value, which if used in a particular way will yield products with a specific value attached to them. In contrast, human resources are frequently seen as an item of expenditure and cost, but infrequently considered from the point of view of their quantitative utilisation and contribution to the business. This view of human resources is important because personnel costs in many organisations are the largest single item of expenditure. Human resources are probably also the one asset of a business which has the greatest potential for improving its contribution to the success of the enterprise. This view is supported by the frequent comment from employees at all levels that they are constrained by the organisation from contributing as much as they might do.

This chapter reviews the role of manpower development in business and the way it might be enhanced through the use of Behaviour Technology.

THE ROLE OF MANPOWER DEVELOPMENT

Much manpower development activity is an act of faith by managers that it is a 'good thing' to develop people. While this may be laudable, it emphasises that the true benefits of manpower development are rarely, if ever, properly assessed. Our perspective when considering the development of people will be that it is an investment in the most valuable asset of the business; its human assets. It is an investment which, if wisely used, will enable people to contribute more productively towards the achievement of organisation objectives.

Improving the contribution made by human resources is not merely a means of increasing short-term profitability. Of equal importance is the fact that the demands of the future frequently involve changing skill requirements. Advanced manufacturing methods introduced over a relatively short timescale have very considerably reduced the amount of semi-skilled assembly labour required in many automobile and domestic appliance manufacturing plants. This manufacturing revolution has also dramatically increased the need for highly skilled technicians to introduce and maintain the computer controlled equipment and processes. Another area where skill profiles have altered dramatically is in chemical process plants. Oil refineries built within the last four years require less than a quarter the number of personnel to produce the same amount of oil as those built only ten years ago. Even the skill requirements for employees in offices have changed, as witnessed by the secretary or clerk who frequently need to know how to use a word processor, calculator or even a computer terminal as well as a typewriter.

Skill requirements at professional and management levels have also changed. One of the effects of the current recession has been to force business organisations to increase the amount of effort they are giving to sales activities, merely to retain their market share. The oil crises since the 1970s have made energy a much scarcer resource and in consequence, the effort devoted to planning the use of energy as well as its conservation have grown enormously. At an information processing level too the requirements for human handling and utilising of data have altered significantly as a result of the impact of computers, especially micro computers.

Wherever we look, the skill needs of industrial organisations are altering. Anticipating and meeting these changed human resource require- ments is no simple matter. While schools, colleges and universities have altered their curriculae to meet some of the needs of industry, a large proportion of employers are having to provide existing employees with these new skills if they are to meet the company's requirements. So manpower development, as well as improving the existing talents of individuals, is concerned with the creation of new skills unheard of only a few years ago.

To fulfil this function, manpower development is dependent on (a) evaluation of the skills of existing employees, and (b) prediction of future skill needs. Without these activities, manpower development would take place in a vacuum. Unless assessment of existing skills is undertaken, it is unrealistic even to attempt to develop these or add on new skills. Before sending an employee on a problem-solving development programme, we need to identify that he really has a need in this area. Improving problem-solving skills might be useful but it may not assist the organisation if the prime reason why job performance is ineffective is that departmental meetings are a shambles. The cause of employe ineffectiveness may have nothing to do with problem-solving skills at all but may, for example, be due to poor relationships with the boss, unclear demarcation of responsibilities between departments, or any of a number of other reasons.

The other prerequisite for developing employee skills is forecasting future skill needs. For example, many organisations traditionally invest resources in training apprentices, as it is assumed that the skills acquired over the three or more years of training will be beneficial to the business. In the days when craft skills were the mainstay of the business this may have been appropriate, but few organisations today can effectively utilise craft skills on their own. The requirement of many manufacturing organisations tends rather to be for adaptable semi-skilled labour, or alternatively for technicians who have much higher skill levels than those provided by a traditional apprentice training scheme. The minder of a computer controlled machine tool is unlikely to find much use for knowledge of how to set up a non-automatic lathe or grinding machine. Apart from the routine operation of the machine, such as loading materials and switching magnetic tapes, the operator needs little knowledge of how the equipment operates. When a fault develops in the equipment, a skilled engineer will be summoned to attend to the problem, which may be an electrical or mechanical fault of considerable complexity. The value of craft skills in automatic manufacturing plant are therefore limited.

For a business organisation to survive it is increasingly vital that it evaluates the skill needs of the future, especially those dictated by changing technology, and plans to meet them. Failure to adapt to this challenge has already prevented many organisations from competing effectively in the marketplace. One of the main tasks of the manpower development specialist is therefore the specification and planning of how future skill needs can be fulfilled.

EVALUATING EXISTING SKILLS AND PERFORMANCE

The conventional process of evaluating employee performance is through performance appraisal mechanisms. From an appraisal it is hoped to identify the particular strengths of employees and also those areas where improvement is required. The Behaviour Technology method of identifying existing job performance deficiencies has already been discussed in Chapter 6. We shall now consider the usefulness of appraisal schemes for assessing an employee's potential to move to other jobs which have different behaviour and performance requirements from their present job.

The final part of many company appraisal schemes considers the future career prospects of the employee. Invariably this takes the form of an assessment by the employee's current manager from his or her knowledge of the way the employee performs his current role. Not surprisingly, therefore, employees who perform well in their current roles are rated as having considerable potential for the future and those who are not deemed to have performed so satisfactorily are considered to have less potential.

From a manager's point of view this may seem logical. If your subordinate appears competent and effective it would appear appropriate to consider him or her for better things, while if they appear less effective there are fewer reasons why they should be promoted. But from a manpower development perspective this assessment may be invalid, as is shown by the fact that so many excellent salesmen prove to be ineffective when promoted to sales manager roles, and many able technical specialists seem incapable of managing other people performing similar tasks.

The reason why so many employees with excellent performance records fail at a more senior level is that the behaviour and performance requirements in the more senior job differ significantly from those in their previous job. The classic example of this is in selling where the skills needed by an effective salesman differ from those needed by a sales manager. While the salesman may require initiative, sensitivity, persuasiveness, tenacity and a lot of Free Child behaviour, these qualities may not assist in, and may even detract from, performing the sales manager role effectively, as the latter position may instead require leadership, planning, management control and a great deal of Adult behaviour. Not surprisingly, therefore, the salesman who displays flair in the behaviours required for selling may well find himself out of his depth when attempting to use the same behaviour patterns to perform a sales manager's role, and so his promotion may prove a disaster for both himself and the company.

Increasingly, companies need employee assessments which can be used to determine transfers to jobs with different performance requirements from employees' present jobs. One very effective vehicle for this is the assessment centre (discussed in Chapter 9), which has particular benefits because the assessment can be made on a totally different basis and independent from current job performance, so it can be used to assess behavioural potential which may be required at some considerable time in the future. For instance, when recruiting graduates many organisations increasingly look for leadership and planning skills, although these are likely to play a relatively small part in a graduate's early career. When the graduate moves to more senior roles, however, these behaviours will become increasingly essential for effective job performance, so it is useful to be able to assess an individual's long-term potential at an early stage. Thus the assessment centre approach differs radically from selection methods which base promotion decisions on the opinion of an employee's immediate supervisor, who may not even need the behavioural skills which the employee will have to display in a more senior job.

Another method which can be used to identify potential to move into jobs with different performance requirements from the present role is through psychological tests. These are especially useful for the assessment of problem analysis and judgement skills. Assessments of intelligence, verbal reasoning or numerical skills are all indicators that an individual has the potential to undertake problem analysis and make judgements based on data. Personality tests may also provide some indication of whether an individual has the potential to fulfil various performance requirements. Many organisations have been able to improve the quality of selection and promotion decisions through the use of psychometric tests, but this approach suffers from the fact that the assessment is of necessity indirect, being derived from the individual's performance in responding to the artificial questions and problems which make up the test. Psychometric assessment also involves difficulties when we attempt to use it as a basis for development, for while it can highlight an overall development need, this will be on a generalised level with little concrete information from which to identify the precise behaviours required to improve an employee's performance. In comparison Behaviour Technology data from an assessment centre or well designed interview can identify the precise behaviours which the individual needs to develop.

ANALYSING AND FULFILLING FUTURE REQUIREMENTS

Identifying future manpower development requirements is a haphazard activity. While existing manpower needs can always be assessed by reference to established jobs, the identification of future requirements necessitates informed judgements about the conditions which will most likely prevail in the future. Undertaking such assessments is one objective of manpower planning. It is contingent on an accurate forecast of the organisation's business plans, and also on how changing technology will influence the way these plans are implemented.

The nature of products and services an organisation plans to provide in the future, and in what quantities, determine the basis for the numbers and types of skilled employees required to fulfil these plans. As many organisations have discovered in the last decade, the products offered to the marketplace in the past are no longer sufficient to ensure future survival. If a company changes from producing typewriters to producing desk-top computers and word processors, the skills required in marketing, sales and manufacturing are likely to change.

As well as the nature and levels of business activity, the manpower planner also needs to anticipate the effects which changing technology will have on how this activity will be undertaken. The importance of changing technology can be illustrated by reference to examples in the electronics industry. Until very recently, the repair of electrical products, whether colour television sets or computers, has required high levels of electrical/ electronic skills. Increasingly the repair of such products is being reduced to a simple standardised routine. If your colour television breaks down, the repairman will quickly check which of a number of circuit boards is faulty and then replace it. If this fails to cure the fault he will suggest you buy a new model. A similar revolution is about to take place in the computer field. Whereas the service and maintenance of computer equipment in the past has been a highly skilled job, it is increasingly being reduced as a result of technological advances to a routinised activity not dissimilar to that of the colour television repairman. Diagnosis of faults on computers is already being carried out over the telephone, with the customer simply linking his faulty machine to the supplier's fault diagnostic computer. This can identify the precise problem and then tell the repairman which circuit board needs replacement. In consequence the skill levels required by computer repair engineers are rapidly decreasing. Instead of being able to diagnose and then rectify a fault, the repair engineer of tomorrow will simply need to know how to replace specified circuit boards. A smaller number of very highly skilled engineers will be required to design the fault diagnosis systems which the repairman of the future will use to undertake this type of fault diagnosis.

From this example we can see how even when the type and level of business activity has been specified (computer service and repair) the skill levels required to carry this out can be influenced dramatically by technological change. The key to analysing future skill requirements is an understanding of imminent changes in technology and an appreciation of how they will influence the structure of jobs in the future. So anticipating future manpower requirements depends on an assessment not only of the movement of employees in and out of the business and the future level of business activity, but also of how business activities will be tackled as a result of technological change. Failure to address these problems has already resulted in a number of large organisations being driven out of business.

The way in which the engineering division of a British multinational company approached the problem is noteworthy. The division had demonstrated to the satisfaction of senior management in the company that advanced manufacturing methods could make a valuable contribution to survival and profitability. The point was well demonstrated by investment in a new factory of computer-controlled machine tools and other automated plant which gave the business much greater responsiveness to the marketplace, and also a return on capital of over 40 per cent per annum, at the same time reducing the number of employees from over 1500 to less than 500.

As a result of this spectacular success, senior management in the division led by the manufacturing director and the head of engineering wanted to apply this approach to business problem-solving throughout the 7000 employees located on fifteen sites. After analysing the issues they concluded that the behavioural requirements for the future lay in the following areas:

1. The adoption of radical thinking in business problem-solving, particularly as influenced by lateral thinking (problem analysis and Little Professor behaviours).
2. Development of the will to succeed and not to be satisfied by marginal improvements in methods, output, market share, etc. (Free Child behaviour, avoidance of Adapted Child behaviour, and achievement motivation).
3. Awareness of the threat of competitors' action, in particular learning from the lessons of increasing Japanese dominance of world markets (problem analysis, judgement, planning and organising, and Critical Parent behaviours).
4. Improved collaboration of employees working in teams to tackle business problems (team working, leadership, initiative, and problem analysis).

The result of this diagnosis of development needs led to the creation of a unique development event which lasted four days. The highlight of the workshop was when competitive teams worked to devise radical solutions to real problems encountered in the business. The output of these workshops was such that a number of new products and processes were designed which were subsequently patented, while others with far-reaching shop floor implications were implemented directly.

The important theme of these workshops was the adoption of new behaviours to meet the challenge of accelerating technological change. Before tackling the major business project on each workshop, participants were bombarded with a series of experiential learning events, including lateral thinking and new team working techniques, as well as information about how leading competitors worldwide were attacking the marketplace. The latter concentrated on the impact of Japanese work methods, including radical redesign of products, robotics, and the impact of aggressive marketing policies. These ideas, many of which were totally new to those attending the workshops, were presented not as ideas in themselves, but as very practical solutions which had direct relevance to the participants' place of work.

In many ways these workshops embodied the spirit of Behaviour Technology (even though I was not aware of this at the time). Throughout the workshops, participants were encouraged to apply new work behaviours to solve problems encountered in their workplaces. Instead of the experience being remote, participants developed practical solutions to business problems which they later had to present to the general managers of the businesses in which they work. This reinforced the acquisition of the new behaviours and especially problem analysis, Free Child behaviour, team working, judgement, management control and Critical Parent behaviour. By the time participants left the workshops, they had not only started to use these behaviours but had demonstrated to themselves and senior management how relevant and appropriate these were to solving real business problems.

Although the computer-controlled machine tool was a critical piece of technology for this company, there are many other technological changes on the horizons of world industry which have equally far reaching consequences on employees. The impact of computers has, for example, only just begun to be felt. We are only a few years away from the time when virtually every manager will have to use a computer on a daily basis for the majority of information purposes. Terminals for receiving business information are commonplace in many businesses and are used in functions including finance, marketing, manufacturing and personnel. The recent introduction of 'Prestel' in Britain already makes it possible for television viewers with this facility to gain access to over 185,000 pages of information from almost 1000 different sources at the press of a few buttons. The information can be updated by the minute and presents a taste of how the computer revolution will affect the home and office. The advent of Prestel is merely a start of the office revolution. In ten years' time the written memo could well be totally obsolete. The technology for all inter-office messages to be flashed up on screens linked to individual storage and processor capabilities is already available. Facsimile machines now make it possible to reproduce detailed technical drawings on the opposite side of the globe in a matter of minutes. If current trends continue it is feasible that the office of the future will be in individual employees' homes. Rather than go to the office each morning, managers might sit at their own home computer terminal which provides them with access to all the information they may need, including direct access to robot-operated manufacturing plants. Going to the office might only become necessary when we wish to see people face to face on occasions, when a view phone is insufficient.

In the manufacturing plant of the future, many employees will be replaced by machines as robots tackle not only spot welding and some assembly work as at present, but virtually all aspects of the manufacturing cycle. A similar but more simple revolution has already occurred in agriculture where the number of farm hands required to operate a farm of a few hundred acres is no more than two or three. A few hundred years ago, several dozen men were required to achieve less output.

The increasing pace of technological innovation has dramatic repercussions for employees and specifically for the performance and behaviours required from them. Whereas traditional techniques of changing behaviour were sufficient to meet the needs of the past, radical approaches are needed if organisations and the individuals within them are to keep pace with change. Behaviour Technology provides a framework with which the performance requirements of the future can be specified and compared to existing employee behaviour. Only when the specification has been produced can development and training techniques be devised to bridge the gap between current behaviour and the behaviours required in the future, and this is considered in the following section.

DEVELOPING EMPLOYEE BEHAVIOUR AND PERFORMANCE

The difference between the current behaviour of employees and the behaviour required to meet present or future needs will be referred to as the 'behaviour and performance gap'. This can be classified in the language of TA and the Problem-Solving Dimensions. The performance gap for a salesman might be a lack of persuasiveness or a lack of Free Child ego state behaviour. The gap for an accountant might be lack of attention to detail or an overemphasis of Adapted Child and Critical Parent behaviours. Whatever the type of behaviour deficiency of an employee, this can (with the exception of those purely related to technical or professional knowledge) be expressed in terms of TA and the Problem-Solving Dimensions.

Once the behaviour gap has been identified, line managers and development specialists can select the most effective method of overcoming it. Traditionally, the process of management development has become synonymous with attendance on a training course. Experts, either within companies or working in external management colleges, provide a myriad of training courses; from a review in 1980, I identified external training courses in the UK designed to overcome almost every conceivable behaviour gap, as defined in terms of the Problem-Solving Dimensions.

One of the advantages of training courses is that the employee is taken out of his or her normal working environment in order to concentrate on the behaviour gap the course is designed to overcome. This enables the trainee to put aside day to day work pressures which might otherwise interfere with learning. While this facilitates the learning itself, it tends to suffer from difficulties in transferring new skills back into work behaviour. This is a problem with T-Group training which, while it heightens individuals' sensitivity to their own behaviour, is frequently not transferred back into the workplace. Similar problems occur with technical skills training, e.g. in computers, finance, engineering, etc. When the trainee returns to work full of new ideas about how to improve things, they may receive the cold shoulder from colleagues. After a few weeks of this the once inspired employee forgets his or her new-found behavioural repertoire and returns to their previous ways of doing things.

Another way of developing employees at work is through coaching and counselling. The two activities are frequently considered synonymous but are in fact very different. Counselling can be seen as the process of giving advice to employees on the options facing them so that they can take more informed decisions about the future. Behaviour Technology can be of considerable value in this as it provides a framework with which the counsellor can explain the various options in specific behavioural terms.

Coaching is much more directive and usually consists of job guidance between a manager and his subordinates. Typically, it might involve the manager in setting up work situations for the subordinate, encouraging him to deal with these, and then reviewing how the employee performed. An example of coaching might be when a manager gets his subordinate to chair a meeting; the manager may ask the subordinate questions which encourage him to handle the situation, and then later review how he coped with this. For example, he might ask his subordinate how he would structure a meeting and how he would deal with particular individuals or issues. A coaching discussion might go like this:

Boss: How will you open the committee meeting?

Subordinate: I'll welcome everyone and then overview the agenda items, before going on to agree the minutes of the last meeting.

Boss: Okay, and how will you deal with Fred if he interrupts as he usually does?

Subordinate: Well, I'll try to avoid arguing with him but will try to divert the discussion back to the issues, and I'll re-emphasise the objectives we are trying to achieve.

Boss: Good. Do you recall the ego states Fred uses when he interrupts? How could you continue to respond with a parallel transaction?

Subordinate: Oh yes, Fred always uses his Adult and therefore I will respond with my Adult.

Boss: When Fred says something like: 'Mr Chairman, this is all rubbish, what we must do is tackle the problem in this way and the reason you can't do it your way is . . .', is that in fact Adult or is it another type of behaviour?

Subordinate: Now that you mention it, I suppose Fred does use a lot of Critical Parent.

Here the manager is reviewing a future meeting and considering in detail the behaviour of his subordinate and the others who will attend the meeting. The benefit of Behaviour Technology here is that it provides a detailed and comprehensive framework with which expressed feelings can be analysed as well as problems solved rationally.

Team development is another behaviour change technique which, in many ways, is a halfway house between attending a formal training course and on the job coaching. The important feature is that employees experience it together with their work colleagues, usually away from the normal place of work. Again the frameworks of the TA ego states and Problem-Solving Dimensions can be used with great effect as vehicles for giving and receiving feedback. Once managers understand the frameworks, they can appreciate what is going on when one manager puts up an Adult proposal (based on problem analysis and judgement) and a colleague starts raising a series of curt and abrupt queries about it (on the surface also Adult but in practice Critical Parent, and probably playing the game of Yes But).

Another application of Behaviour Technology is in the formulation of career structures and streams. Career structures are made up of a series of jobs at successively higher levels in the organisation, through which individuals can move as their careers progress. Without even using the term career structure, many organisations already conceive certain jobs as forming a career structure — for instance in the academic world, lecturers move on to become senior lecturers, then principal lecturers, and ultimately readers and professors. This is the case in many organisations, both those of an authoritarian type such as the army or police force and those with a less rigid structure such as research laboratories.

The benefits of TA and the Problem-Solving Dimensions is that they can be used as criteria for specifying the behaviours required for success at the various positions in a career structure. Both selection and development decisions can thus be made in a more systematic manner than would otherwise be possible.

A fundamental problem facing many manpower development activities is relating the requirements for skills to the development methods used. In the past, managers often defined the behaviour gap in one set of terms while the people responsible for implementing development activities used another, altogether dissimilar, one. This caused misunderstanding and confusion, as well as leading to development events which failed to satisfy the original identified need. This problem need no longer exist and as a result the effectiveness of manpower development can improve markedly.

11 Managing conflict

Conflict is an emotionally loaded subject. While it may conjure up images of large-scale struggles between unions and management it is an ever-present feature of organisational life at all levels and pervades much of what we do irrespective of our function, role or status in the business. The conflict that exists between sales and production in many companies is only one example of the inherent nature of conflict in organisations. In this case the conflict is usually due to the very different perspectives of the two functions; while sales tends to be predominantly outward looking towards the customer, production tends to be inward looking towards maximising the use of existing resources.

Conflict also characterises the relationship of an organisation with its environment. While customers place particular demands on a firm, e.g. for delivery against specific price and performance standards, the business may well attempt to modify these to suit its own profitability objectives. Firms experience the reverse situation with their own suppliers, who may attempt to modify the demands placed on them to fit in with their own needs to achieve economies of scale, profit, standardisation, etc. Relations with the community and government officials also frequently involve conflict. While the community may attempt to impose certain standards such as pollution control and equal opportunity of employment, the organisation may often attempt to evade these requirements so that they interfere as little as possible with the achievement of organisational objectives and values.

Relationships within organisations are also characterised by conflict. Different departments in the organisation pursue different and sometimes opposing objectives. While the personnel department may want to run a particular management development programme, finance may put on pressure to curtail all but the most vital forms of expenditure. Conflict abounds within departments, between bosses and subordinates and between peers who are competing for the same scarce resources.

Conflict is an ever-present phenomenon of every organisation, but it may be managed in such a way that its effects are less destructive that they might be. After all, the majority of supplier—customer negotiations between firms result in contracts which more or less meet the needs of both supplier and customer. Most union complaints and disputes result in settlements with management which do not threaten the survival of the organisation, even though the personal interests of many employees do not coincide with the priorities set by their bosses. Although characterising organisation life, conflict is usually managed and resolved through well established processes and mechanisms. Only when these mechanisms fail do the results of conflict, such as strikes or legal actions, hit the headlines.

This chapter will examine some wider conflict issues and some methods of conflict management used in business organisations, and how they can be made more effective with Behaviour Technology.

THE BENEFITS OF CONFLICT

The media frequently bring to our attention the destructive consequences of conflict, and it therefore seems appropriate that we should first consider some of the actual benefits that can arise from conflict. Whether we consider conflict between two individuals or between large organisations (including nation states), it may give rise to three important benefits.[1]

The most immediate benefit is that it can help to readjust the relationship of the parties concerned. If circumstances change, as they are doing increasingly rapidly in today's turbulent society, this can radically affect the position of one party and so have far-reaching consequences for the parties' relationship. It is significant that the recession has altered relationships between labour unions and large employers in many countries. Whereas in the mid-1970s many employers found themselves desperate to attract and retain employees, this is certainly not the case today. Many companies today find themselves in a buyer's market and can negotiate advantageous wage rates much more easily than was possible a few years ago. This is particularly demonstrated by some American multinationals which, in 1981, imposed rate reductions or standstills on their employees in an attempt to cut losses brought about by the recession. We can view these wage settlements, which were strongly resisted initially by organised labour, as examples of how the relationship between management and unions has altered through conflict, with the power balance between them shifting away from the unions towards management.

On an individual level, a manager who is promoted within a business will subsequently find that his relationships with others who previously were at the same level are different because they are now in more subordinate roles. While they may originally have been in direct conflict when competing for resources, this is likely to alter when the manager rises up the organisational pyramid; conflict is likely to take a different form when the former colleague raises issues and problems with the new promoted superior.

Behaviour Technology can help us, whether at an organisational or individual level, to become more aware of our relations with others in terms of problem-solving and expression of feelings. When the relative power positions of the parties in a relationship alter, they can more quickly appreciate what new behaviour is appropriate to the changed situation. In union-management relationships there is now more emphasis on controlling wage rates and on cost effective deployment of manpower. Accordingly, problem analysis and judgement behaviours by management have tended to increase in the area of wage bargaining, and large organisations can now express more Critical Parent towards labour and less Adapted Child. A similar change is also likely to occur in the individual who finds himself senior to colleagues who previously were on the same level.

Another benefit of conflict is that it can help to emphasise boundary relationships. If production and sales find themselves in conflict, one of the effects of this will be to emphasise and clarify the role and function of sales for sales people and equally to clarify the role of production for production departments. The emphasis of boundaries as a result of conflict is frequently noticeable in international relations. Britain's success in the 1982 Falklands crisis has resulted in the British people feeling greater pride in their country and more sense of national purpose. The side-effects of international conflict in improving a nation's cohesion are a well-known phenomenon which politicians have exploited. Hitler did so effectively for the Germans in the 1930s, Churchill for the British in the Second World War, and Mrs Thatcher and her party are now reaping the political benefits of 'successful' warfare just as Napoleon did in France a century ago.

From a Behaviour Technology perspective an emphasis on boundaries can be viewed in part as a greater awareness of one's own objectives and goals and an increased belief in the value of one's own position. This leads to a kind of pride which is very much a feeling of 'we are the good guys', 'our side is the right one', which originates from the Critical Parent ego state.

The third possible benefit of conflict is as a safety valve. Efforts can lead to the build-up of frustration and tension, especially if we do not achieve our goals. Conflict with another individual or group can act as an outlet for this tension and so prevent it from contaminating everything else we do. This is particularly noticeable in union–management negotiations, when each side may go through a phase of expressing totally negative feelings about the other. Union officials castigate management as incompetent and exploiters of workers, while management complain that union officials want to ruin the organisation and are influenced by political extremists. So long as this expression is controlled and each party tolerates the other's outburst, they can afterwards get down to business to solve the real problems between them. Union—management negotiations frequently depend on whether this ritualistic expression of hostility between the parties can take place without either party becoming rattled or upset. If inexperienced negotiators take the outbust to heart and react, the resulting hostility can create a considerable setback for the ultimate achievement of an outcome which is satisfactory to both sides.

From a TA viewpoint, expression of negative feelings is often a Child behaviour, for instance an expression of rebellion against authority and perhaps against one's own Adapted Child ego state. Giving vent to hostile feelings can, as is well known by therapists, be a useful first step in developing awareness of a problem so that ultimately it becomes possible to move on to constructive problem-solving. This may be impossible if our negative feelings remain bottled up.

REAL AND APPARENT CONFLICT

Although conflict is an inevitable part of organisational life, it frequently does not lead to beneficial outcomes of any kind but is on the contrary unproductive and wasteful or even positively destructive. Newspaper headlines almost daily proclaim the latest industrial disputes where unions and management are locked in a battle of wills or where rival corporations dispute a takeover bid. In these and similar types of conflict the process can become very heated, and each side may take actions which may well be to the ultimate detriment of all parties concerned. The fact that destructive conflict occurs so often suggests that this is an area which managers need to understand better.

Most conflict has its roots, at least in part, in some difference of attitude or goals between the parties involved. While union officials may believe that their members deserve a 10 per cent increase in pay, company management may believe that the most the business can afford is 5 per cent. Although sales believe that customers need to have delivery within two weeks of placing an order, production may regard lead times of one month as essential for achieving economies of scale. A boss may believe the task he has given to a subordinate is realistic and achievable, while the subordinate may consider either that it is the wrong task and that to undertake it is not in the best interests of the organisation, or that is quite impossible to achieve within the given constraints. Such differences may constitute the basis of conflict between parties. However, once developed, the original issues in dispute become much wider. Union officials come to regard management as exploiters who are wilfully trying to prevent employees enjoying a fair standard of living, while managers may perceive the unions as being led by political extremists who are bent on bankrupting the company. Sales consider production as a conservative group of plodders who do not know what life outside the factory gates is like, while production in turn see sales as a 'loudmouthed bunch' who do not understand the product and spend their time lavishly entertaining customers. The boss sees his subordinate as lazy and rebellious while the subordinate views his boss as incompetent and outdated in his thinking.

As conflict develops the parties involved tend to view their antagonists in a different light. Instead of confining conflict to the issues in dispute, we begin to perceive our opponents in a totally negative light and attribute hostile motives to them. This process develops until we forget the original issues and concentrate instead on the all-embracing nastiness of the other party; in this situation concrete issues are no longer important in themselves but are used as weapons against our opponent. The real issues are ignored while the apparent issues dominate the relationship.

At an objective level it may appear easy to stand back and separate the real from the apparent issues of conflict. However, from the point of view of each party, the apparent issues become critically important and inseparable from the real issues. The struggle between the Catholics and Protestants in Northern Ireland has all the signs of being dominated by apparent issues, the real issues of conflict having been to a large extent forgotten.

Behaviour Technology provides a framework we can use in a very practical way to separate the real from the apparent issues in a conflict. The real issues concern facts, data and objectives and relate to the Problem-Solving Dimensions and the Adult ego state as well as to Free Child wants and needs. The apparent issues of conflict will contain expressions of Critical Parent judgements (as opposed to Adult data) or Free Child expressions of hostile rebel feelings.

If we have a stereotype that our boss is an outdated conservative, we can ascertain whether this is a judgement from our Critical Parent or a conclusion drawn as a result of rational problem analysis and judgement. Both the verbal and non-verbal communication coming from our Adult ego state would be considerably different from how the same opinion would be expressed by our Critical Parent ego state. The statement, 'The boss is really useless, all his thinking is weighed down by the past. He is a hopeless case left over from the last century,' contains considerable Critical Parent judgement, as illustrated by the words 'all his thinking', 'is really useless', 'left over from the last century'. It contrasts with the more Adult sentence, 'My boss is not interested in new ideas and whenever I put a suggestion for change to him, he puts up all sorts of reasons why it should not be implemented.' While the first sentence contains only judgements the second contains data about the behaviour of the boss. While the individual who perceives his boss as typified by the first statement is likely to experience considerable apparent conflict, one who sees him as typified by the second is more likely to be dealing with the real issues of conflict.

career development prospects and special company benefits such as cars. Shop floor operators in contrast have less attractive terms and conditions. While these differences in reward may contribute to real conflicts, they may also lead to apparent conflicts if inappropriate conclusions are drawn from the differences in reward. If managers' terms and conditions are seen as unfairly distributed, the real differences in reward may be exaggerated, thus leading to apparent as well as real conflict.

Role differences between departments, as well as between levels or subsections of an organisation, can also be a cause of both real and apparent conflict. While production may correctly view personnel as being rule bound, they may also perceive them as bureaucratic and negative.

METHODS OF MANAGING CONFLICT

Since the 1950s, various organisation experts have grappled with the problems of resolving conflict. Considerable effort has been put into laboratory studies where conflict has been purposely developed in order to identify practical steps that can be taken to overcome it. The results of these investigations have led to approaches which attempt to reduce the apparent conflict between parties by allowing them to realise that issues of this type are based on faulty perception rather than reality. Once the apparent issues have been resolved, the rational efforts of the parties can be concentrated on tackling the real issues.

One overriding factor which influences whether parties in conflict can resolve their differences is their overall approach to conflict. It has been found that if conflicting parties *believe* their differences to be irreconcilable they are unlikely to make progress in resolving them. On the other hand if the parties believe that a degree of collaboration can help them to achieve their respective objectives, they are much more likely to be able to develop joint solutions which at least partly meet the needs of both. The extent to which this is likely to occur can be summed up by whether the parties perceive conflict as leading purely to win/lose outcomes or to possible win/win outcomes. If parties in conflict believe they can only achieve their objectives at the expense of the other party, their implicit approach is that they can 'win' only if the other side 'loses'. This approach is referred to as a 'win/lose' strategy. Alternatively, if the parties believe that they are most likely to achieve their own objectives if the other also achieves something, their implicit approach is one of collaboration; this is called a 'win/win' strategy and makes joint problem-solving possible.

The significance of adopting win/lose or win/win strategies towards conflict is that they have completely different implications for the behaviour of the parties towards each other. Adopting a win/lose approach implies that each party views itself as superior to or better than the other (which is a Critical Parent behaviour), and is likely to indulge in Free Child behaviours of a negative kind towards the other. There is then little scope for using the Adult ego state to solve problems.

In contrast, when win/win strategies are adopted the parties are able to listen to and understand the needs of their opponents. There will be less Critical Parent and angry Free Child behaviour, which will allow the Adult ego state to take over and use the appropriate Problem-Solving Dimensions to identify and work on the real differences separating the parties. Some of the dimensions which can help to resolve conflict are interpersonal sensitivity, problem analysis, flexibility, planning, and attention to detail.

Expert negotiators use strategies which involve a mixture of behaviours. In many negotiating teams there is a hostile role which involves behaviours of the win/lose variety which put pressure on the opposing party. A different individual may then apply win/win behaviour strategies which involve working with the other side instead of against it. Combined together in various ways such negotiating tactics can lead to a solution which meets the needs of all the parties involved. These successful solutions include cases where suppliers and customers sign a mutually advantageous contract and when unions and management agree a workable wage settlement. Such solutions may not hit the headlines as do those cases where conflict results in open hostilities between the parties because they are incapable of coming to an Adult agreement, but it is such agreements which keep the wheels of industry turning and allow a reconciliation of parties with different interests.

The following interchange between a union official and a department manager may help to clarify the differences between win/win and win/lose methods of handling conflict:

Union official: I understand you've victimised one of the lads. Your supervisor has just sacked John Andrews and I want this withdrawn right now or there'll be real trouble.

Manager: Don't tell me how to do my job, Joe. John Andrews was sacked yesterday for misconduct and if you had been on site, you would have been informed in the usual way.

Union official: Don't give me excuses. I want John reinstated today or I'll bring the shop out. I'm not joking.

Manager: The man's been sacked for a very good reason and I'm not going back on the decision —

Union official: Right, that's it. I'll have the place stopped this afternoon.

Manager: Just a minute, Joe, do you know why we sacked John Andrews?

Union official: Another case of victimisation. I know the supervisors, if they don't like a bloke they give him the push.

Manager: We did inform the other union's representative on the section and he even saw John Andrews yesterday. The man was drunk,

absolutely incapable of operating a machine safely, and we gave him a
final warning three weeks ago about being drunk on duty.

Union official: You're exaggerating. Just because a bloke breathes a few
beer fumes, you call him drunk. That really won't wash.

Manager: Apart from ruining the work on his machine and leaving it
unminded, he collapsed on the floor. If that isn't drunk, then I don't
know what is.

Union official: That's fiction . . .

Manager: Have you talked to the supervisor in charge of the section or
any of the lads? You might also want to discuss the matter with the
nurse who had to attend him.

Union official: Prove it.

Manager: Look, don't take my word for it. Go and talk to the other lads
John worked with, and also to the supervisor. The only reason you
weren't informed was because you were off site yesterday, otherwise I
would have called you in to see him for yourself.

Union official: I have my doubts. That supervisor in charge of the section
had it in for John.

Manager: Can I suggest you have a word with the other lads on the section
and with the nurse? They all saw John. Let's discuss the matter again
when you've seen them. You might also want to talk to the representative from the other union who was called in as an independent witness.
You may remember that we gave John a final warning last time he was
drunk and you were present when that happened.

Union official: I'll be back.

Manager: I'll expect you and be happy to talk it through with you when
you've seen everyone who witnessed what happened.

The initial five interchanges between the union official and the manager
are win/lose in their approach to one another. The union official wants
John Andrews reinstated and the manager is sticking to his decision to
sack him. For the union official to have got his way (win), the manager
would have to go back on his decision to sack John Andrews (lose);
alternatively, for the manager to stick to his decision (win) would have
meant that the union official would not achieve his demand to have him
reinstated (lose). In his opening statement, the union official is displaying
angry Free Child behaviour: 'I want this withdrawn right now or there'll
be real trouble.' The manager responds with Critical Parent behaviour.
'Don't tell me how to do my job,' and then with Adult behaviour: 'if you
had been on site, you would have been informed in the usual way.' The
crossed Critical Parent transactions continue as the two men fail to
communicate with one another. The manager then switches to his Adult
ego state with: 'do you know why we sacked John Andrews?' This is an
attempt at introducing some problem analysis and judgement into the

transaction. However, the union official merely responds with more Critical Parent behaviour: 'I know the supervisors . . .'. The manager uses more Adult behaviour in response to this: 'We did inform the other union's representative on the section and he even saw John Andrews', which is problem analysis and also refers back to the previous incident when he was drunk and was given a final warning (which was a piece of management initiative and control in case his drunken behaviour was repeated). The conversation continues, with the manager using Adult behaviour and the union official using gradually less Critical Parent behaviour, eventually agreeing to go and talk to the witnesses of the previous day's incident.

Besides introducing more Adult behaviour into the situation, the conflict between the two has shifted onto another plane. The two are no longer locked into a win/lose conflict but have moved towards a win/win situation in which the union official agrees to check up on whether the manager's contention is correct so that they can both resolve the matter. Without reference to the facts, i.e. the real conflict, the two would have continued to be locked in apparent conflict. In this case the apparent conflict involves the union official's view that supervisors victimise workers they dislike and the manager's view of the union official as an interfering nuisance who is challenging his right to manage.

While the above example may appear straightforward, in practice it is difficult for the parties in conflict to move away from the apparent issues to grapple with the real ones. Conflict-solving involves the parties in disengaging from the apparent conflict issues over a period of meetings and then examining the facts which separate them from one another. Such procedures involve both parties in developing awareness of how they are seen by their opponents and then managing to convey the inaccuracy of these perceptions. External parties to the conflict can be useful in encouraging the process and facilitating real problem-solving. From a Behaviour Technology perspective, these approaches amount to a reduction of Critical Parent and angry Free Child behaviours and an emphasis on Adult behaviours. By concentrating on the Adult ego state, each party is able to clarify their own position (leadership) and undertake planning and organising, problem analysis and judgement in collaboration with the other party. It is also helpful for the parties to clarify the issues they have in common and this entails joint leadership. Focusing on joint objectives and goals has been referred to as the creation of 'superordinate goals' in the literature.[2]

Conflict is an area where Behaviour Technology can make a real contribution. When we are involved in conflict it is easy to become so engrossed in our negative evaluations of the other party that they dominate our entire behaviour. The way to overcome this is not by some magical formalised process but rather by a practical approach which we can use to develop awareness of ourselves and others. Feelings, including hostile feelings towards others, are real and form part of our inner world. Rather than deny these negative feelings and beliefs, we need to take responsibility for them and realise the implications they have for our transactions with others. In the above example the manager initially behaved in a negative Critical Parent manner towards the irate union official, with unproductive results, but when he later adopted a different ego state towards him the two were able to examine the real issues involved in the situation rather than their negative feelings towards one another.

As conflict is an inherent aspect of all organisational life, between bosses and their subordinates, between different departments and functions, not to mention between members of different organisations, our own effectiveness depends on becoming competent at conflict management. Behaviour Technology provides a foundation stone for this by helping the parties involved to become aware of their own and the other side's behaviour, thus separating the real from the apparent issues of conflict and allowing conflict-solving options to be developed.

REFERENCES

1) Coser, L., *The Functions of Social Conflict*, Free Press, 1956.
2) Sherif, M. and Harvey O.J., *Intergroup Conflict and Cooperation*, University of Oklahoma Press, 1961.

12 Implementing Behaviour Technology

Successful implementation of Behaviour Technology depends on whether the organisation will derive real benefit from it. This may sound like a truism; after all, when companies introduce automated manufacturing methods they do so to increase the volume of output and reduce work in progress or labour ccsts, and equally when computers or office automation are introduced this is aimed at speeding up information processing or improving management ability to control the business. Unfortunately the same does not always hold true with many human resource techniques and processes that have been launched in unsuspecting organisations. The record of contributions made by many fascinating manpower development techniques, including interpersonal skill training, leadership development programmes and intricate selection practices, leaves more than a little to be desired. It is not so much that these techniques *cannot* contribute to the organisation, but rather that in too many cases their contribution is, at best, intangible.

The principal requirement for introducing Behaviour Technology is that it should assist achievement of wider organisational strategies and objectives. Just as no two people are the same and no two organisations are identical, the needs and priorities of one organisation will be different from those of another. Consequently, the implementation of Behaviour Technology cannot be achieved in a standardised, uniform manner but should rather take place in a way which relates to the priorities of the business. This may well mean that Behaviour Technology is introduced to different employee groups, and for tackling different types of human resource problems, in different organisations. While it may be used mainly to develop management leadership skills in one company, it could be utilised to enhance the selection skills of supervisors in another. The overriding requirement is that Behaviour Technology is implemented only where it can directly help the organisation achieve business objectives.

The second requirement when introducing Behaviour Technology is that full account should be taken of its concern with the objective facts of what people actually *do*. Unless those using Behaviour Technology to tackle specific organisational problems are able to pay sufficient attention to the realities of behaviour, implementation will become academic and meaningless. This chapter addresses these two requirements and shows how Behaviour Technology can be introduced in ways which both take account of organisational objectives and give a central place to ascertaining the facts of behaviour. We will concentrate on the second requirement first.

HOW TO EXAMINE BEHAVIOUR

Many of the basic skills we rely on in life, such as being able to read and write, do simple arithmetic, or drive a car, were learnt as a result of systematic training. This training was conducted over a period of time, mostly under the supervision of a skilled trainer. Schoolteachers in most countries in the Western world have to pass examinations before they are let loose on the citizens of tomorrow. Even driving instructors need to be members of recognised institutes or gain government approval before they can teach this skill to others. Ironically, very few people have received formal training in the gathering of behavioural information, although this too is a basic life skill. We need it in any management or supervisory role as well as when selecting a mate, bringing up our children or developing friendships. But not only did we receive no training at school in this skill, we probably received none at university either unless we happened to study psychology or a related discipline. The only training most managers ever get in gathering facts about others is during short interpersonal or interviewing skills programmes.

The first requirement when introducing Behaviour Technology into an organisation is to provide those involved in its application with systematic training in gathering behavioural information. The process, outlined in the chapter on assessment centres (Chapter 9), involves four steps: observation, recording, classifying and evaluation. Only when employees have acquired reasonable skills in these four activities can they become competent at harnessing behavioural data to solve specific business problems.

Basic training in the skills of observation, recording, classifying and evaluation (ORCE) can be given in a three-day training programme involving simulated job situations which are familiar to the participants. If the trainee population were salesmen, a typical simulated situation might include the problems encountered by a salesman with a customer, while a performance improvement discussion between a sales manager and a salesman might be used for a group of sales managers.

The training situations could be usefully derived from assessment centre job simulation exercises. Many such exercises have already been developed by consultants, particularly in the United States, and these would provide ideal training material. The exercises could be conducted prior to the training programme by role players and be recorded on videotape for playback during the programme. Alternatively the job simulation exercises could be conducted live during the course, giving trainees the opportunity to record live data as it occurs. Each approach has benefits and drawbacks.

Pre-recording of a job simulation for use in a training session enables the trainer to carry out his own prior evaluation of the material, against which trainees' performances can be compared. This frees the trainer to devote more attention to the trainees themselves rather than to carry out his own assessment during the programme. It also makes it possible to provide a model behaviour assessment for candidates' use while watching the job simulation so that they can then better understand how the process works. The drawback of previously recorded material is that it does not have the freshness and immediacy of live behaviour. It suffers from the selected field of vision of the television camera, whereas in real life, when two people are talking across a table there will be other things going on apart from the facial expressions and the words themselves — one person might be tapping their hands on the table, for instance, or crossing and uncrossing their feet. These may well be significant pieces of data. A final drawback of pre-recorded material is that the trainees may not feel involved in it, as none of them is participating. Using live material makes it possible to provide a fuller field of vision for trainees and also to use data provided by the trainees themselves for evaluation. This will increase participants' involvement in the training process, thereby reinforcing the acquisition of skills.

The first half of a basic training programme in ORCE might involve four or five practice sessions in which participants carry out the complete process of observation, recording, classifying and evaluation of material. In earlier exercises pre-recorded materials might be used and then once trainees have a reasonable grasp of the process they might conduct live exercises of which they themselves were involved as role players in the job simulation.

In such a behaviour assessment training programme either the Problem-Solving Dimensions or Transactional Analysis should be used. To attempt to learn both frameworks simultaneously in a short training course could well confuse trainees. The framework used for training will be dictated by the particular organisational applications where Behaviour Technology will be used by participants; more will be said about this later.

Each practice assessment session would commence with trainees observing a job simulation lasting half an hour and recording as much information about what was actually happening as possible. The emphasis will be mainly on verbal behaviour, with some record of non-verbal behavioural indicators if TA is used. After the job simulation candidates would classify and evaluate the observed behaviour from their own recorded data, according to either the Problem-Solving Dimensions or the TA ego states and transactions. They would then meet together with the trainer to discuss their evaluations and the facts on which these were based. Normally the trainer will invite one participant to lead the discussion on a particular behaviour factor, i.e. one Problem-Solving Dimension or one of the ego states. The other participants will compare their own assessments with this and the trainer will clarify the issues emerging from the discussion and point out where inaccurate assessments and classifications have been made. Reference to a recording of the live session or to the original pre-recorded material during this discussion can be especially useful for reinforcing learning and clarifying problem areas.

The training programme is most effective if the latter part of it concentrates on the application areas where it is intended to use Behaviour Technology. While this part of the programme may not need to be particularly detailed, it is essential that trainees appreciate why they are being taught behaviour assessment skills. Thus if the main objective of introducing Behaviour Technology is to improve selection interviewing, the latter part of the course should focus on this and alternatively if the objective is to assist managers to improve their negotiating skills with trade union officials or suppliers, this area should be featured. Even though separate training programmes may be used to provide Behaviour Technology application skills in specific areas, it is important when teaching assessment skills that the reasons for this are well understood and appreciated.

Unless participants appreciate that the skills they acquire have real value in helping them achieve their work (or personal) objectives, they are unlikely to put much effort into acquiring them. This difficulty is encountered on interpersonal skill courses when participants are told to attend by their bosses. The positive benefits of attendance may never be explained to the subordinate, while the boss has arranged for them to take part in the pious hope that this will cure some personality defect. Under such circumstances, the trainee not surprisingly may become suspicious about the whole experience, and as well as resisting learning anything from the course he may even attempt to disrupt the whole event. After experiencing such participant reactions I adopted the approach of asking all participants on interpersonal skills training courses why they were there and how they hoped or expected the course to assist them at work. Despite the embarrassment this question caused to more than a few participants it brought the problem out into the open, thereby allowing the individual participant and the tutor jointly to tackle this all-important question.

Precisely the same applies to behaviour assessment skill training programmes. To gain the commitment of trainees it is essential to provide a clear indication of how they can use their newly acquired skills in a positive way once they leave the training environment. Failure to address this issue can make the acquisition of such skills little more than an academic exercise.

A particularly useful way to address this problem is to use job simulation as well as teaching assessment skills specific to the areas where Behaviour Technology is to be applied. Thus if the objective of introducing Behaviour Technology is to develop selection interviewing skills, the simulations might include behaviour assessment of actual interviews, while if it was planned to use Behaviour Technology for appraisal then the situations might include appraisal discussions. Where the objective is to improve leadership or group working skills, the simulations used could be group discussions in which a leader either was or was not appointed. Similarly the content of the discussion itself should also be relevant to the participants. For sales managers, the job simulation with maximum impact would involve actual sales problems, for example campaign tactics or account planning, as well as discussions between, say, a salesman and his manager about how the salesman might improve his performance in this area. In the case of personnel specialists the training situations might include an actual job interview. In this way the job simulations used for teaching assessment skills would be relevant to trainees from an intrinsic content point of view as well as from a situational perspective.

DEVELOPMENT WORKSHOPS

Another way of introducing Behaviour Technology into an organisation is to assist employees to develop their own managerial skills. Rather than just enabling managers to acquire behaviour assessment skills, they can be encouraged to do so while examining their own situation. This approach has proved to be successful in ICL and has helped the Problem-Solving Dimensions to become part of the organisation's language while at the same time developing individual managers. The approach depends on managers becoming aware of their own strengths and development needs.

These development workshops usually lasted five days, the first day and a half being devoted to participants tackling a series of assessment centre exercises which were recorded either on tape or video. The job simulations covered various management situations, e.g. a group discussion, a problem-solving exercise which involved information gathering, a one to one interview between a boss and subordinate, and an in-tray exercise. The remainder of the workshop then involved each candidate assessing the performance of others from audio and video tapes and receiving feedback on their own performance from others. Armed with this comprehensive feedback, participants were then able to identify overall areas of strengths and development needs.

From these workshops, managers acquired a number of important benefits. The most basic skill and the one on which all the other learning hinged was skill in assessing and evaluating behaviour, and in addition they acquired detailed feedback on their own personal performance. As a result of such events, employees have been much more able to select career paths which capitalised on their own personal strengths and which did not draw undue attention to those areas where performance was not so effective.

The development workshop involved a number of steps which assisted the acquisition of assessment skills. Rather than merely telling another participant that his or her performance was effective, employees were required to give specific examples which supported this evaluation. Even if a participant's performance was rated as satisfactory, this implied that while there were examples of effective performance there were also others which were less effective.

One of the drawbacks of the development workshop is the tendency for participants to revert to assessments which converge towards the median of the scales. One strategy for encouraging assessors to notice effective as well as less effective performance is for them to identify three Problem-Solving Dimensions in which the participant is specially effective and three where performance is least effective. In this way each participant, over the course of the workshop, obtains a large volume of information about where they are most and least effective, and from this some overall pattern can usually be expected to emerge. Irrespective of overall levels of performance this leads to the identification of areas of particular strength as well as areas of weakness.

The development workshop possesses more potential than any other method I know for highlighting individual development needs in the Problem-Solving Dimensions. While we all have some ideas about our personal work behaviour, the material on which these are based often tends to be anecdotal or attributable to conclusions drawn from some incident in our experience. In contrast to these ad hoc methods of feedback, the development workshop is able to provide much larger quantities of verifiable data, so that participants can see themselves in action and understand how their problem-solving behaviours affect the results they achieve. Realistically, participants can expect at least three examples of their behaviour to be identified on each of the dimensions assessed at a workshop. Multiplied over five exercises, this would give fifteen concrete pieces of data. Because of the structure of the workshop, assessor bias (both positive and negative) can be reduced substantially by having different assessors observe and comment on each participant for each exercise. If consistent behaviour and performance assessments are made by different assessors, and in different job simulation situations (e.g. in-tray, one to one discussion, and group discussion), the validity of the accumulated material is likely to be high.

A necessary preliminary to setting up a development workshop is to identify the relevant job behaviours required for success in participant's jobs. There would be little point for example in using 'initiative' as one of the Problem-Solving Dimensions for junior managers in a stable bureaucracy. In most bureaucratic organisations, initiative among junior managers is likely to be regarded as a dysfunctional behaviour rather than the opposite. While initiative, persuasiveness, and interpersonal sensitivity may be highly relevant to sales personnel, these dimensions are likely to contribute much less to success in an accounts department.

Use of Transactional Analysis in a development workshop can also be very stimulating. The need here is less prescriptive and more to encourage participants to identify through their own experiences the types of behaviours which best contribute to specific situations and problems. In sales situations, it has been found by many firms that Free Child behaviours (within the norms of business situations) can play a major part in clinching a deal. If the customer likes you and trusts you (Free Child reactions) he or she is much more likely to buy from you. On the other hand, successful selection interviewing will tend to use mainly the Adult ego state combined with some Nurturing Parent behaviour; the Adult will help to seek out information about the candidate while the Nurturing Parent will help to put him at ease. Use of large amounts of Free Child behaviour would tend to make the interviewer less impartial about the candidate while Critical Parent behaviours will inhibit rather than encourage a free flow of information.

In appraisal or disciplinary situations, a degree of judgement is required in addition to information-seeking of a logical kind. Consequently, Critical Parent behaviours will need to be used. In management situations a variety of different ego states, stroking behaviours and transactions will be required. Because inevitably we each have our preferred ego state behaviours (you may have identified some of mine by now!), training and development will involve learning to adapt these to the requirements of the situations in which we find ourselves.

Because of the profusion of feedback available, it can be useful to provide participants with opportunities of changing their behaviours during the workshop itself. If for example a participant identifies that he has development needs in the areas of planning and organising, leadership and initiative, he could attempt some of the job simulations for a second time while concentrating only on these behaviours. This would require a large number of tutors in the final stage of the development workshop to coach participants in the behaviours they are trying to develop. Alternatively, candidates could learn from one another; the participant with a development need in planning and organising might receive coaching and feedback from a participant who had particular strengths in these areas.

Behaviour practice in terms of TA ego states, transactions and stroking patterns can also take place in a development workshop. Participants who display considerable Free Child behaviour can act as models for those with deficiencies in this department, and so on. This technique encourages behavioural change through the three main methods by which this can occur: conditioning, modelling and self-development.

Because of time and resource constraints, it is usually not practicable to use both TA and the Problem-Solving Dimensions on the same development workshop. Because the two frameworks are so different, it may be better to develop the two types of behaviour in different events — both together might overwhelm participants in even a two-week programme. The framework which is considered most relevant to the planned application of Behaviour Technology should be adopted, and only at a later point should the second be grafted into the culture of the company, if appropriate.

APPLICATION RELEVANCE

Effective introduction of Behaviour Technology depends on it forming part of the total human resource plans of the organisation. While considerable discussion takes place about this lofty concept, in practice relatively few businesses at present generate such plans, let alone implement them in practice. As a guide to the types of Behaviour Technology applications which may be of value to particular organisations, the following sections review the human resource needs of organisations of three different types: expanding organisations, those under threat, and those operating in stable environments. While I know of no perfect method of categorising organisations, the three types do appear to reflect the possible stances of most businesses in the industrial world.

THE EXPANDING ORGANISATION

The human resource requirements of expanding organisations are critical, especially when the rate of growth is rapid. While the expansion of a business can lead to significant improvements in market share, profitability and ultimately stability of the organisation, it can also be fraught with human resource problems — so much so that industrialists have, on many occasions, commented that the biggest obstacles in times of growth concern human as opposed to other resources.

While it is difficult to generalise across industries and sizes of expanding organisations, certain human resource characteristics appear to be common to growth businesses. The most obvious of these is the need for additional employees with the required skills to meet expansion needs. Another requirement is for work methods, processes and structures which are different from those already established.

Before additional employees can be obtained to meet expansion needs, it is necessary to define their required skill profiles. When a company gets larger it usually will not require more staff in all functions and levels, but rather only in certain job roles. The profiles of skills and experience needed may differ from those already in the organisation if new technologies and methods of working are to be adopted. Rather than applying to one-off jobs, it is more likely that defined performance requirements will apply to complete families of jobs, e.g. application software specialists, salesmen and maintenance engineers for a computer company; semi-skilled CNC machine tool operators and planning engineers for a consumer manufacturing business; clerical staff with computer terminal operator skills and branch managers for a bank.

Besides taking on new staff from outside the business, expanding organisations often have an acute need for experienced staff from within who have the potential to fulfil new supervisory and management positions. This places considerable pressure on promotion systems and management development activities. A feature of expanding organisations is that they frequently do not have sufficiently experienced employees to take up the new opportunities that arise. This creates a need to evaluate existing employees' potential to cope with new jobs for which they may not have directly relevant experience.

The main contribution of Behaviour Technology to expanding organisations is in external and internal recruitment and selection, much of it concerned with the assessment of future potential. For this purpose the interviewing methods described in Chapter 5 and the assessment centre techniques described in Chapter 9 can be used. Considerable effort will also need to be directed towards management development and the development workshop mentioned earlier is likely to be useful here.

Another need of expanding organisations is for individuals who can adapt to working in new structures and with new technologies. Small expanding organisations tend to create new centralised functions, then, after further expansion, these are decentralised and more staff are taken on in operating divisions and units. Still further growth often leads to the centre expanding its field of operation and influence, again with more staff being taken on. In this way growth results in changes in organisational structure as well as in working methods and practices, and this will place considerable pressure on employees' relationships with each other. Successive changes often lead to the creation of new work groups and the dissolution of old ones, and because these groups may be shortlived as well as less structured than in more stable organisations, their members will need to have high levels of group working skills. Behaviour Technology development methods can help here, as discussed in Chapters 7 and 8.

THE ORGANISATION UNDER THREAT

For the purpose of this section organisations under threat will be defined as those that find their market and financial position under attack. Usually this will arise from competitors' activities, but can also be due to internal labour—management conflict, supplies shortages which affect competitors to a lesser extent, poor financial management, or simply a falling off of customers' interest in the goods or services provided. Firms in Europe and the United States now find themselves under threat as a result of the higher productivity and market responsiveness of Japanese competition. This, coupled with the effects of the recession, have currently placed many industrial organisations under threat.

Usually, the primary requirement for a threatened organisation is to increase its overall effectiveness. This may take the form of increases in productivity or may involve radical innovation in some area of the company's operations, for instance the introduction of new manufacturing methods or redesign of the product range. From a human resource point of view both these improvements involve existing job holders performing their jobs better. In many organisations this has involved manpower reductions so that the current workload is handled by fewer employees; this can be done by identifying those employees who contribute least to overall effectiveness and either help them to perform better or enforce their departure. Appraisal schemes which focus on current job perform-ance rather than on potential for the future are particularly useful in such situations, and schemes based on Behaviour Technology are likely to prove efficient for this purpose because they allow employees to be assessed in a more objective and impartial manner than might otherwise be the case. As a result better decisions, whether concerning dismissal or guidance on improving performance, are likely to be made. The development workshop approach described earlier can then be used to improve the performance of job holders.

The behaviours appraised and developed in organisations under threat are more likely to be the Problem-Solving Dimensions rather than those described by Transactional Analysis. It is not that TA behaviours do not affect business performance — quite the reverse — but rather that these behaviours tend to have an indirect effect. In times of threat a firm is more likely to concentrate on behaviours which contribute immediately to the task in hand.

Leadership styles and behaviours are also likely to be critical in times of threat. In wartime, military leadership styles, which emphasise Critical Parent behaviours and the dimensions of decisiveness and management control, are valued both in and out of the armed forces. Evidence from large companies which successfully come through periods of threat suggests that a similar phenomenon may occur in their leadership behaviour. For instance the styles of the managing directors of British Leyland, British Steel and ICL all appear to be more autocratic than those of their predecessors.

While the development of managers' leadership skills may not be high on the priority lists of organisations under threat, it appears to be a central issue under these circumstances. Behaviour Technology provides a framework which can be used to change and develop leadership styles by helping the practising manager to evaluate his own style and assess its impact on others. Special leadership training and development experiences can then be devised to assist managers in acquiring the skills needed by their organisations.

If conflict is the main cause of the firm's threatened position, it is essential that the individuals concerned should become better equipped to cope with it. The clearest example of this situation is when industrial disputes between unions and management disrupt the ability of the organisation to operate normally. The conflict may be over direct issues such as wage rates, or over more complicated issues such as the introduction of advanced technology — cases in point are the British newspaper industry and British Rail. In America it has until recently been a significant characteristic of the automobile industry. Japanese industrial organisations, on the other hand, are renowned for their absence of internal threat; both wage rate negotiations and new technology introduction appear to take place in a generally harmonious atmosphere.

Behaviour Technology can assist in the management of conflict as it can provide insights into the positions and behaviours of the parties during negotiation, and also help in planning strategies and tactics. Conflict workshops involving external interventions based on Behaviour Technology could also be of benefit.

THE STABLE ORGANISATION

At present there appear to be fewer organisations operating in stable environments than was the case in the past. Nevertheless there are still a number of such organisations, including government and quasi-government bodies and certain monopoly or oligopoly businesses. Such organisations tend to be bureaucratic in their mode of operation and dominated by established procedures and rules about what can and cannot be done.

Individual success in bureaucratic organisations is determined not so much by the extent to which an employee contributes to the overall performance of the organisation, but more by their ability to operate within the rules. Consequently the definition of performance requirements for individual job roles is essential in this type of organisation.

While stable organisations will not need to take on as many new employees as expanding businesses, they will nevertheless experience a continual requirement for new staff and will also have to pay some attention to career development for existing staff. Selection devices based on Behaviour Technology, including interviewing and assessment centres, can make a useful contribution here. Their particular benefit, as is demonstrated by the British Civil Service Selection Board type of assessment centre, is improved accuracy of assessment of potential for success in this type of organisation.

One of the recurrent problems encountered by large organisations is alienation of employees, especially at more junior levels.[1] Without attempting to review the vast literature on this subject, a basic component in this alienation seems to be the apparently meaningless nature of many junior jobs in bureaucratic businesses. Such jobs make only limited use of individual abilities, take no account of the needs of the people performing them, and often appear to have little connection with the overall aims of the organisation. As a result they strike the individual employee as both meaningless and demeaning.

While Behaviour Technology cannot provide any instant solutions to overcome the monotony of boring jobs, it can be used as a vehicle for predicting which jobs are likely to be the most monotonous and dull from an employee's perspective. It can then be used to restructure jobs in order to make them more meaningful to employees and more useful to the business.

Of the three types of organisation considered, stable organisations will obtain least benefit from Behaviour Technology. The main reason for this is that both expanding and threatened organisations involve changes in human resources, whether in quantitative or qualitative terms. Behaviour Technology, like other technology forms, is a method of bringing about change, and therefore in situations where change has a low priority the benefits to be derived from it are likely to be less.

Implementing Behaviour Technology in an organisation cannot be achieved by any textbook methods. Although some general guidelines on the more important issues involved have been considered, any application should be related to the human resource priorities of the individual organisation. If these have not been identified in the wider context of total business plans, then implementation of Behaviour Technology is likely to be a hit or miss affair at best.

REFERENCE

1)   Beynon, H., 'Working for Ford,' Harmondsworth, Penguin, 1973.

13   Wider issues in Behaviour Technology

It would be a mistake to think of Behaviour Technology as a magical cure-all, a kind of healing and stimulating ointment which can be rubbed into managers' brains like hand cream to leave them miraculously alert, perceptive and resourceful. This kind of panacea may be desirable, but it has yet to be invented. Although it cannot provide instant solutions to human resource problems, Behaviour Technology does set out a conceptual framework which can be used to diagnose and understand problems and to plan and implement practical solutions to them. In common with other technologies, Behaviour Technology holds that there are no ultimate truths or infallible techniques, but that through paying attention to the available evidence the most appropriate solutions can be identified. I hope that Behaviour Technology, like other technologies, will continue to develop and evolve new and more effective methods of achieving its aims.

In contrast to many other forms of technology, however, Behaviour Technology has relevance for everyone who works in an organisation. While only a few employees in a manufacturing company need to know the details of computer technology or mechanical engineering, anyone who is involved in influencing others can obtain benefits from Behaviour Technology. Whether we are concerned with managing a large department or advising others as a consultant, we will be more effective if we can become more aware of others' behaviour. This will help us to deal with their idiosyncratic tendencies and reactions in day to day life, and also to develop strategies and tactics for influencing them on more important issues. Through developing a better understanding of one another, the combined efforts and energies of everyone in an organisation can be better integrated towards the achievement of organisational objectives.

Despite its usefulness, the introduction of Behaviour Technology must take account of other factors and issues which influence organisational life. This final chapter considers the ones that seem important to the author.

INDIVIDUAL AND ORGANISATIONAL VALUES

Behaviour Technology aims to improve wealth creation activities. While this goal is largely shared by the managers and shareholders of commercial organisations, in some cases it may not be the most important objective. Different cultures and societies value different things; in Japan the need to save face, or in the West the desire for freedom of choice, may become more important than wealth creation. The application of Behaviour Technology must therefore take place in the wider context of culture values and goals.

An inherent feature of all current technologies is that they evolve and develop. The solutions that were effective at one time cease to be appropriate later on. The impact of rising energy costs has, for example, made the five-litre gas guzzler car totally obsolete. The impact of the microchip has made the valve computer and radio of the 1950s into industrial antiques. So besides valuing wealth creation, technology — including Behaviour Technology — will also implicitly value constant change and evolution.

Reaction against the two implicit values of wealth creation and change have at times resulted in technology being rejected or at least slowed down. The Luddite riots in early nineteenth-century England involved the smashing of newly installed equipment in the first factories. The reasons for this were complex, but certainly included a rejection of the social change brought about by industrialisation, including the redistribution of wealth and the dehumanisation of working life. More recent resistance to new technology is perhaps well illustrated by the anti-nuclear lobby. Despite the alleged world shortages of fossil fuels, many people in the West believe that the potential benefits of nuclear technology are outweighed by the threats it poses for the health of citizens, not to mention the global hazards of the proliferation of nuclear weapons. This is not the place to evaluate the arguments for or against the peaceful application of nuclear technology, but it is significant that the anti-nuclear lobby has caused multinational corporations and national governments to become more cautious in its application.

Another area where resistance to technology has been significant, even if low-key, is in the field of advanced manufacturing. In Europe and America, the adoption of automated manufacturing methods such as robotics has been much slower than in Japan. This is despite the fact that much of the equipment originated in the United States. Part of the reason for this has been the resistance of organised labour, especially over fears of unemployment. Another reason, usually less publicised but probably as important, is management resistance. Managers with vested interests fear the repercussions of new technology for their own empires and ultimately for their own job roles and status in the organisation.

So resistance to the introduction of new technology is a common experience in many organisations, and may well occur over the introduction of Behaviour Technology. While its positive benefits will probably be valued by managers, it does nevertheless challenge the way in which many managers think about people and human problems. The challenge posed by Behaviour Technology is perhaps best illustrated by the initial reactions and difficulties encountered when it has been introduced into organisations.

DIFFICULTIES IN APPLYING BEHAVIOUR TECHNOLOGY TO DATE

Perhaps the most controversial application of some of the principles of Behaviour Technology is in T-groups or in sensitivity training. The aim of a T-group is to develop participants' effectiveness through receiving feedback on how others perceive and react to them. The group usually meets for a number of consecutive days and is largely unstructured, with most of the time being spent focusing on participants' feelings and behaviours in the 'here and now'. During the group participants have an opportunity to try out new methods of behaving and responding to others which can become the basis of permanent behavioural change. Although a leader participates in the group, his or her main objective is to concentrate discussion on the 'here and now' rather than on abstract ideas. Apart from reminding the group of this, the leader will generally not attempt to interfere with the process of the group.

Since their first use in the late 1940s, T-groups have aroused and continue to arouse intense debate. One of the reasons is the alleged adverse effects groups have had on some participants. Rigorous investigation of such possible cases, however, suggests that this is largely a myth.[1] The doubts expressed probably concern the operation of the group itself, which goes against the rules of most societies about how we can expect to interact with others in group situations. In all but a few sub-cultures it is very unusual to be permitted to tell others exactly what we think of them without such frankness being regarded as hostile, as it is to experiment with different forms of behaviour. This is precisely what occurs in a T-group and consequently it can create anxiety and tension.

In contrast to Behaviour Technology, most T-groups use everyday terms to describe members' behaviour. Nevertheless, the processes of T-groups involve many of the same principles as Behaviour Technology. Both, for instance, concentrate on individual behaviour. Even though this is done in an open-ended way in T-groups, the feedback received leads many participants to re-evaluate and then change their methods of interacting with others, which is also an objective of Behaviour Technology. The main difference between the T-group approach and Behaviour Technology is that the former generates awareness of behaviour in isolation from the workplace while the latter is more structured and can therefore be more readily applied to specific interactions encountered in organisations.

Behaviour Technology has been adopted in training programmes designed to improve effectiveness in specific situations. Particularly popular are courses aimed at improving skills in public speaking, selection interviewing and appraisal. Programmes in these areas now commonly provide a simulation of the situation where performance is to be improved, and give feedback either from other participants or tutors or increasingly from closed circuit television. Feedback is usually given in a structured format applicable to the training situation. Thus in public speaking courses feedback might be given on a candidate's speech volume, projection and speed/tone variation; in selection interview training courses the feedback may concern listening as opposed to talking time, use of open and closed questions, and avoidance of leading questions; while programmes to improve appraisal skills may emphasise the mutual discussion of problems, concentrating on problem-solving rather than on personality traits, and the formulation of future targets and objectives. This kind of situation-based training programme is now common in most large organisations and is largely considered to be beneficial. Its main drawback is its very specificity. Unless participants encounter similar situations shortly after experiencing training, the odds are that much of the course learning will be forgotten and may never be used when finally they do encounter the situation in question. The framework and language used to evaluate behaviour is situation-specific and therefore not relevant to other situations; the use of public speaking criteria in a discussion between a boss and subordinate may well be irrelevant, as may be the use of selection interviewing behaviours in a public speaking situation.

The advantage of Behaviour Technology is that the framework of the TA ego states and transactions and the Problem-Solving Dimensions can be used in a variety of different situations, as shown in previous chapters. This considerably widens the scope and relevance of the Behaviour Technology method of behaviour classification.

The principles on which Behaviour Technology is based have also been used by a multitude of approaches to improving group working. The pioneering work of Bales, and that of Coverdale and Honey, referred to earlier in Chapter 7, hinges on providing feedback to individuals working in a group so that they can adopt new, more appropriate behaviours for increased effectiveness. Although it is difficult to generalise about these many approaches, each tends to use a unique language to describe group behaviour, and often the languages are concerned only with task activities or only with expression of feelings. The extent to which they cover both these fundamental aspects of behaviour is limited.

Despite these criticisms, group work training programmes (irrespective of the precise framework used to evaluate behaviour) are aimed at developing understanding of individuals' behaviour and increasing their options for behaving/reacting differently. In contrast to situation-specific training courses, improving effectiveness in group working can often apply to other life and work situations. Adopting more appropriate behaviours in a group can assist us in managing or chairing meetings with subordinates, contributing to interdepartmental meetings and collaborating in project teams. The skills acquired can also be helpful in our personal lives, for instance in our participation in social organisations, in sports or leisure groups, in enjoying parties more and even in getting on better with our families. As a result of attending such programmes, many of us have learned useful things about ourselves which have later proved to be of practical value.

The above review barely does justice to the many possible applications of Behaviour Technology in organisations. It will be apparent that Behaviour Technology is hardly a new approach; on the contrary, it has evolved over the last thirty years as an established method for developing individual effectiveness. However, the benefits derived to date from applications of Behaviour Technology are still only a fraction of what they might be. This is because such applications have mainly taken the form of isolated one-off events. Because the specific behaviours studied at training courses are not part of the universal currency of organisations, they are gradually forgotten and ignored, and so have little long-term value for either the individual or the business. Other non-trained colleagues cannot reinforce the learning, which, even if retained, is only applicable to specific situations. Perhaps the best indication of the low level of success of most applications of Behaviour Technology is that they are generally limited to training situations. Only when Behaviour Technology is fully integrated into organisational life, in the same way as other forms of technology are, will it be reasonable to claim that it is being successfully used.

OTHER ORGANISATIONAL FORCES WHICH CONSTRAIN THE INTRODUCTION OF BEHAVIOUR TECHNOLOGY

Introducing Behaviour Technology into an organisation constitutes a major organisational change. The introduction of any new technology requires reallocation of resources and new methods of working, whether it be computer technology, automated manufacturing or Behaviour Technology. Before embarking on such a major venture we will want to be clear that it really will contribute to the achievement of organisational objectives. When computers become a viable business technique for storing and processing information in the late 1960s, a few organisations were quickly able to exploit the technology for their own benefit; other organisations remained aloof, and yet others found that the benefits originally promised by computerisation failed to materialise or were balanced by unforeseen disadvantages. The lesson to be drawn is that the introduction of new technology is not in itself a guarantee of success, and this applies as much to Behaviour Technology as to computers.

Two conditions must be met if the introduction of Behaviour Technology is to be meaningful. The first is that significant improvements in the performance of individual job holders will really help the organisation to survive and achieve its goals. The second is that the value and power system prevailing in the organisation is compatible with the implicit assumptions of Behaviour Technology.

At first sight it might appear obvious that improvement in the performance of individual employees will have a positive effect on the achievement of organisational aims. Close inspection of some organisations, however, suggests that factors other than individual performance are more critical for success. The results achieved by some organisations are in fact more dependent on the environment in which they operate than on whether their employees are highly effective or merely marginally effective. This applies particularly to many monopoly or oligopoly organisations, where their dominance of the market is the most critical factor determining the achievement of organisational goals. In such cases, a 20 per cent improvement in the effectiveness of all individual job holders may contribute less than a simple product price increase of 10 per cent. An increase of 10 per cent in world petroleum prices could be expected to contribute more to the profitability of multinational oil companies than very substantial improvements in the effectiveness of their employees. Similarly the profitability of banks is very significantly influenced by changes in interest rates, and the high levels will contribute more to the profitability of these institutions than almost any change that could be introduced from within the business, whether computers or Behaviour Technology. A similar situation applies to speculative house builders in many countries, whose profitability depends more on the inflation of private home prices than on the performance of individual employees; during the boom times of the mid-1970s the profits of home builders in the United Kingdom soared, while the dramatic slowdown and even decrease in house prices in 1980/82 created a very lean time for the industry.

The second prerequisite for introducing Behaviour Technology is that it must be compatible with established value and power systems. In many organisations this may not be the case. The framework of Behaviour Technology requires the establishment of a language within the organisation with which employee behaviour can be understood and analysed, and this language describes observable facts rather than abstract assumptions about what people do or think. This perspective may seem obvious and straightforward, but in fact it may well conflict with the established value and power system. If major decisions tend to be made by those with the best information, and actual performance is the predominant criterion on which individuals are evaluated, then Behaviour Technology is likely to be compatible with the values of the business; but there are other ways in which key decisions are made, and other criteria on which individuals are evaluated.

Power in an organisation can stem from a number of different sources. While expert knowledge is one source, it can also result from personality, position, or resources. In some organisations, power can stem from the personal influence or charisma of key individuals. What they say goes, irrespective of whether it is reasonable, valid or even in the interests of the business. In such cases, if a manager with high personal power evaluates an employee negatively, this assessment (with all its implications) prevails irrespective of the facts. If the manager bases his assessment on his own personal liking or dislike for the employee rather than on any objective assessment of performance, the role of Behaviour Technology in assessing the individual's abilities is likely to be less significant than the simple gut feeling of the powerful manager! In this situation, Behaviour Technology would conflict with the dominant mode of decision-making and exercising power in the organisation and therefore be difficult to implement.

Most of us at some stage during our careers will have come across particularly powerful individuals whose impact was derived more from their personality and charisma than from any objective contribution they made to the organisation. This applies especially to family firms or ex-family firms.

Another source of power can be the possession of resources. Decisions concerning the allocation of resources to individuals are often at least partly accidental. It is not uncommon to find senior managers with large offices, a well groomed secretary in the outer office and an executive car in the car park, who require any expenditure they propose above £500 to be countersigned by someone else. The real power at the disposal of such managers may in practice be minimal, while somewhere else in the organisation a junior member of staff may make strategic decisions affecting the whole organisation, for which they are given no recognition.

An example of this was when consultants were called in to review the effectiveness of a medium sized high technology engineering company known to me. Despite United Kingdom market dominance and a significant world share of their product market the company was not growing significantly, nor was it as profitable as senior management would have liked. As a result of their investigation, the consultants discovered that a clerical supervisor was making decisions which dictated the company's output for up to a year ahead. Because the company depended on bought in components which took between four and twelve months to be supplied, decisions about which components to order were critical. It appeared that for years the clerical supervisor had been committing the company to its production schedules through making decisions about the purchase of these long lead time components; nothing the marketing or manufacturing directors did could override her decisions to more than a marginal degree.

If power in the allocation of resources is unsystematic or haphazard, the actions of a few individuals become more important than any other decision-making or problem-solving method including Behaviour Technology. Only if these people can be won over to Behaviour Technology is its implementation likely to be successful.

Related to resource power is position or procedural power. This involves influencing others by creating rules and procedures. The existence of particular bureaucratic rules in an organisation may be so time consuming and demanding for individuals that they find it virtually impossible to operate (and behave) in any alternative manner. The existence of highly bureaucratic personnel procedures in one company restricted the capacity of individual managers to act, and also prevented the personnel department from contributing to the business. The use of Behaviour Technology for improving the effectiveness of the personnel department was severely constrained by these circumstances. However, when Behaviour Technology became an integral part of the rules for promotion and management development, it acquired a legitimate basis in its own right.

Closely related to power is the value system of an organisation. Roger Harrison[1] has classified the culture or value systems of organisations as being based on power, roles, tasks or individuals. To simplify our discussion, culture will be defined here as the dominant rules of an organisation which dictate what qualities, actions and outcomes are prized and rewarded and which are disapproved of and punished.

In power cultures control is exercised through a few key individuals and decisions are primarily determined by a balance of influence rather than procedures, rules or logic. This is likely to be a resource power dominated organisation in which the key individuals with access to resources allocate them. Such organisations may not place a high value on logic and reason as decisions will tend to be made on the basis of precedent and the disposition of the few individuals with power. The successful application of Behaviour Technology in such an environment will therefore depend on the extent to which the dominant individuals support it. If their support is not forthcoming, the commitment to its introduction in terms of energy and expenditure will need to be very high and the benefits derived will be susceptible to undermining by the key decision-makers.

However, Behaviour Technology is likely to be both valuable and viable in role culture organisations. These function largely on logic and reason and work is distributed according to a predetermined order. The personnel function hires people because the procedures dictate that only personnel can make job offers, and so on. In this type of organisation, if Behaviour Technology is moulded to the existing procedures and role situations it is likely to succeed. The training department will be able to run Behaviour Technology courses because this is their function and equally line personnel departments will be able to make interview assessments or introduce appraisal schemes based on Behaviour Technology because it is their prerogative to do so. Thus the prime requirement for introducing Behaviour Technology into a role culture is its implementation as part of the established procedures of the organisation.

Another type of environment where Behaviour Technology is likely to prove of considerable value is in task cultures. The overriding concern of individuals in this type of organisation is to achieve results. Influence is likely to be widely spread and based mainly on individual expertise and ability. Because the evaluation of individuals is already based on performance, the introduction of Behaviour Technology is likely to be seen as a means to this end. In theory, an organisation with a task culture would seem to be ideal for the application of Behaviour Technology, but in practice such organisations tend to be overlaid with other possible values, e.g. power or role cultures, and these secondary cultures must also be taken into account.

The individual-oriented culture will hinge on the activities of individuals and have minimal structure. Such cultures tend to apply to small professional practices and co-operatives and will not be considered here, where our main concern is with large and medium sized organisations.

LONGER-TERM PROBLEMS IN USING BEHAVIOUR TECHNOLOGY

The use of Behaviour Technology in an organisation is likely to encounter a number of difficulties. Even after a successful initial introduction and implementation programme, as proposed earlier, the technique will face threats concerning its continuing operation.

The biggest challenge facing the use of Behaviour Technology is whether it continues to contribute to business effectiveness and performance. The history of management techniques introduced in the 1960s and 1970s suggests that, after initial impact and value, they were discarded and forgotten. This even applied to intrinsically sound techniques such as management by objectives, leadership training, and problem-solving techniques. The reasons for the demise of many such management tools is often not a reflection of their internal validity. Rather it is because they were introduced to solve specific organisational problems and priorities which, once addressed, led to management effort and attention being focused elsewhere.

The justification for the continued use of Behaviour Technology depends on the extent to which it can be adapted and tailored to tackle changing human resource priorities. While the priority when Behaviour Technology is introduced may be recruitment and internal promotion, the priority two years later may be a change in the balance of employee skills. Later still, the company human resource priority might shift to the management of conflict brought about by a merger with another organisation. Unless Behaviour Technology can be used to respond in a flexible and constructive way to changing human resource priorities there is no business reason why it should continue to be used.

One of the dangers facing the introduction of Behaviour Technology is that it becomes stereotyped as a technique for solving only one class or type of problem. Should this occur, it would not be surprising that as soon as this type of problem becomes less important managers forget about Behaviour Technology. Those responsible for the application of Behaviour Technology therefore have a responsibility to ensure that it contributes to solving problems which are truly relevant. As many organisations began to feel the impact of the recession they questioned the value of long-term management development programmes. Not surprisingly, as the survival of the company came under threat, managers focused on short-term issues rather than on the long term. Quite appropriately many long-term management development programmes were cancelled or curtailed in the early 1980s. The prime target instead became ways of increasing employee productivity in the current year, failing which there might not *be* a 'next' year!

As well as responding to new and changing priorities, Behaviour Technology also needs to be integrated with new human resource approaches and methods. The present popularity of 'Quality Circles' in Europe and the United States is such a case in point. Quality Circles have been acclaimed as a means of improving productivity through increasing work group cohesiveness. Circle members use brainstorming and other problem-solving techniques to generate solutions that can be recommended to management. In Behaviour Technology terms the behaviours involved respectively are Free Child, and Initiative, Creativity, Problem Analysis and Judgement. Rather than perceiving Quality Circles as a threat to Behaviour Technology, the manpower development expert should view Behaviour Technology as a means to assist the evaluation, implementation and direction of specific management methods. If Behaviour Technology is adapted to new methods and approaches it is more likely to continue to be useful to an organisation in solving problems of performance and productivity.

In addition to the challenge from new human resource priorities and new management techniques, Behaviour Technology will also come under threat from the point of view of the resources consumed. Quite appropriately the resources invested in implementing and maintaining the use of Behaviour Technology will come under scrutiny from time to time. The costs of developing new applications and running training courses, not to mention line management effort, all mount up. As well as budgeting the costs, those involved need to assess and evaluate its contribution. While the human resource specialist may consider the costs more than justified, the case needs to be made to line management. Not only should the benefits of Behaviour Technology be rigorously scrutined, but if tangible benefits are obtained these need to be publicised. If for example the use of assessment centres increases the success of management placements these benefits should be evaluated, if possible in financial terms which can be compared with the costs incurred.

Should the use of Behaviour Technology be found to be of questionable value, remedial action needs to be taken quickly. The cause of poor contribution from Behaviour Technology may come either from within the application itself, or because the outputs are themselves not used properly. If a particular application of the method is found to be less cost effective than those used previously it should either be withdrawn or modified. Responsibility for this rests squarely on the manpower development specialist. At one time when I was involved in running assessment centres I realised that participants were not getting sufficient benefit from the activity. To help address this situation we improved the briefing given to participants, so that they knew better what to expect from the centre; we also improved the quality of assessor discussion so that individuals' strengths and development needs were better identified.

The longer-term application of Behaviour Technology in an organisation depends on its wider adoption and integration in many human resource activities. Behaviour Technology might be seen as useful in solving specific problems, but managers should be encouraged to extend the approach to tackling other problems. The implementation of Behaviour Technology into the ICL appraisal system, for example, was a highly cost effective exercise because managers already knew the language of the Problem-Solving Dimensions. Opportunities for such wider applications therefore need to be sought out so that Behaviour Technology language can become as common currency in human resource discussions as the intricacies of hardware and software terminology in discussions on computer systems.

The ultimate requirement when using Behaviour Technology is that its application becomes a means to an end, and not an end in itself. No management technique can become an end in itself — its use must rest on its contribution to organisation effectiveness and performance. If this contribution cannot be made, the use of Behaviour Technology should be discontinued. Behaviour Technology profoundly challenges the ways we look at and deal with human resource problems. In the place of reaction and prejudice, Behaviour Technology proposes that we can tackle and overcome human problems by looking at the facts of behaviour. In the place of models and academic theories, Behaviour Technology proposes that we can explore the options open to ourselves and others for behavioural change. In the place of leaving things to chance, Behaviour Technology can help us to take responsibility for what happens to our lives.

Thus Behaviour Technology poses a serious challenge to current management thinking and action. However positive the conditions, implementing Behaviour Technology will be no easy matter; the practitioner owes it to himself or herself to use the techniques of Behaviour Technology to tackle the issue of resistance to its introduction. Only when this fundamental problem has been addressed does the practitioner stand a chance of achieving more effective management of human resources.

Behaviour Technology is not just a body of ideas. Its value is rather as a practical bag of tools for solving human problems in organisations. For some jobs the tool bag already contains all the necessary items, while for others it might be considered inadequate. The only way to determine whether the Behaviour Technology tool bag is useful is to try it.

REFERENCE

1) Harrison, R., 'How to Describe Your Organisation', *Harvard Business Review*, Sept.–Oct., 1972.

Index